Landscapes *of* Wonder

Discovering Buddhist Dhamma in the World Around Us

Bhikkhu Nyanasobhano

Foreword by Bhikkhu Bodhi

Wisdom Publications • Boston

WISDOM PUBLICATIONS
199 Elm Street
Somerville, Massachusetts 02144
USA

© Bhikkhu Nyanasobhano 1998, 2013

Essay 4, "Nothing Higher to Live For," appeared previously in
the Buddhist Publication Society's *Bodhi Leaves* series.

Library of Congress Cataloging-in-Publication Data

Nyanasobhano, Bhikkhu.
    Landscapes of wonder : discovering Buddhist Dhamma in the world
around us / by Bhikkhu Nyanasobhano.
        p.   cm.
    Includes index.
    ISBN 0-86171-142-4 (alk. paper)
    1. Religious life—Buddhism. I. Title.
BQ4302.N93 1998
294.3'4—dc21   98-17767

ISBN 9780861711420   EBOOK ISBN 9780861718894

17 16 15 14 13   6   5   4   3   2

Cover photo, "Hume Lake Stars," is courtesy of Josue Claros.
Cover design by Tony Lulek.
Interior design by Jennie Malcolm. Set in Bembo 10.75/13.85.

Wisdom Publications' books are printed on acid-free paper and meet the guidelines for
permanence and durability of the Committee on Production Guidelines for Book Longevity
of the Council of Library Resources.

Printed in the United States of America.

 This book was produced with environmental mindfulness. We
have elected to print this title on 30% PCW recycled paper. As a
result, we have saved the following resources: 3 trees, 2 million BTUs of energy, 262 lbs. of
greenhouse gases, 1,420 gallons of water, and 95 lbs. of solid waste. For more information,
please visit our website, www.wisdompubs.org. This paper is also FSC® certified. For more
information, please visit www.fscus.org.

Landscapes *of* Wonder

Table of Contents

Publisher's Acknowledgment

THE PUBLISHER gratefully acknowledges the generous help of the Hershey Family Foundation in sponsoring the publication of this book.

Foreword

At the base of the entire system of mind training taught by the Buddha is a particular orientation toward experience called *yoniso manasikāra*. Though usually rendered "wise attention" or "careful consideration," *yoniso manasikāra* has a penumbra of meanings that makes it stubbornly resistant to translation. The expression points to a mode of attending to immediate experience that marshals astute mindfulness and thorough reflection in a concerted effort to uncover the hidden truth of existence. One who practices *yoniso manasikāra* refuses to be taken in by superficial impressions, by the endearing smiles and bland assurances of sensory phenomena, but pushes on, with keen observation and relentless questioning, until he has reached the underlying bedrock of truth.

The book you hold in your hands is an exquisitely crafted exercise in *yoniso manasikāra*, a remarkable testament to the twin powers of wise attention and careful consideration. On page after page the author demonstrates that he has heeded well the Buddha's message that the key to awakening lies just beneath our noses, that all we need to discern the birthless, deathless face of reality is to attend closely, deeply, and thoroughly to the everyday procession of events. The truth that brings wisdom and freedom does not reside in a mystical domain of its own, sealed off by steel gates from this dreary transient world in which we pass our lives. All along it has been dwelling right here—in our bodies, senses, and minds, in the flow of rivers, the flight of birds, the rhythms of the earth. The task the Buddha sets before us is to probe this material deeply, with unflinching honesty and courage, until we uncover the unvarying, universal laws of actuality. It is these laws that collectively constitute the Dhamma, the Teaching and the Truth, and it is the realization of this Dhamma that extinguishes the flames of our suffering.

In *Landscapes of Wonder* Bhikkhu Nyanasobhano leads us on a voyage of discovery, or rather a series of such voyages, helping us to decipher the cryptic code of Dhamma stitched into our everyday lives, beeping incessantly in the world around us. The book is a collection of contemplative essays covering a wide range of topics related to the Buddhist spiritual life, all written with a command over diction and imagery that is truly exhilarating. The essays fall roughly into two broad categories. One consists of reflections on the problems of practicing the Buddha's teachings under the conditions of modern life. In these essays Ven. Nyanasobhano offers us solid, sober, level-headed advice that ushers us past the mazes and blind alleys awaiting the unwary traveler straight on to the pure, lofty, radiant path to freedom as taught by the Master himself. He does not seek to compromise the teachings to make them more palatable to jaded tastes, but shows us how we can apply the ancient, time-tested guidelines of the Dhamma in the perplexing world of today. Although this mode of writing in itself is not particularly new, Ven. Nyanasobhano's words of counsel on such issues as the enchantment of romantic love, the challenge of renunciation, the demands of moral integrity, the need to respect the Dhamma on its own terms, and the signs of spiritual progress all brim over with sound common sense and uncommon wisdom.

It is with the second type of essay that our author is in a class of his own, master of a genre that is virtually his own creation. This is the contemplative excursion: literary vignettes that are at once bold flights of the imagination and complex tapestries of thought. Having invited us to join him on his saunterings through woods, parks, and fields, he begins with apparently banal observations about the familiar sights we meet—a fallen tree, a swollen river, the colors of the earth, a crane rising in flight, a fish dangling on a line. Then, starting from these humdrum remarks, he subtly leads us through a series of reflections that strip away layer after layer of our cherished delusions until we find ourselves, as if startled out of sleep, staring the raw truth of the Dhamma in the face.

Like fine miniatures these essays compress an enormous amount of detail into a relatively brief compass. They should not be read on the run in the way one grabs a sandwich and a cup of coffee on lunch break; rather, they should be savored leisurely, with frequent pauses for reflection, as one might drink a cup of Chinese tea while watching the full moon march across the sky. I would suggest not reading more than *one* contemplative essay per day. And on finishing the whole collection, read them all again, for they contain so many levels of meaning, such subtle reverberations of insight, that each reading will yield fresh rewards.

I first came to know Ven. Nyanasobhano about twenty years ago, when he was just beginning to develop a serious interest in the Dhamma. Over the next few years his commitment to the Dhamma continued to deepen, even to the point where, in 1987, he entered the Bhikkhu Sangha, the Buddha's Order of Monks. Parallel with his practice of Buddhism his literary gifts have also matured, as he has continued to spin off one essay after another, each showing an increasingly greater mastery over the art of "wise attention." With the publication of *Landscapes of Wonder* I think it would hardly be an exaggeration to say that American Buddhism has at last found its Thoreau, its rambling, loquacious poet-philosopher who can show us the deepest revelations of truth in the woods, rivers, and fields. This is an eloquent, joyous, and uplifting book, written with consummate skill, introducing us to profound new perspectives on the ever-fresh, ever-fecund Teaching of the Enlightened One.

Bhikkhu Bodhi

IN THIS BAFFLING WORLD where human beings laugh and weep and sometimes search for meaning, the voice of the Buddha can still be heard, stirring and uplifting the individual mind. The Buddha attained perfect enlightenment and then taught with such memorable brilliance that his words did not fade but lasted through the centuries, giving hope, light, and inspiration to whoever listened intently and then looked around thoughtfully at the world.

The faith of the Buddhist grows out of experience fortified by instruction. The Buddha shows how to make the journey out of suffering to emancipation, and if we feel a quickening of interest we can take steps ourselves to investigate and to test what we have learned. This collection of essays is about finding the right direction and then moving forward with mindfulness and deliberation.

Questioning people, who are troubled by life's contradictions, want to know why the world goes on as it does and often feel the need for a guiding standard that gives gladness and allays pain. Buddhism answers questions about suffering and about the nature of the noble life here and now. More than that, it offers a healthy course of conduct that leads to peace of mind, understanding, and, eventually, freedom from all sorrow.

When someone has come to regard Buddhism with more than casual interest and feels the attraction of its depths, the obvious problem then becomes how to live this teaching, how to put it into practice in modern situations that seem remote from the times and cultures of its traditional homelands. Fortunately the teaching of the Buddha is universal, giving us the chance not just to admire what others have admired but to make our own search—to observe, meditate, and discover through our own efforts. The passage of centuries and the upheavals of history do not hamper this search, because the laws of nature still operate in us and around us. If we come to a clear understanding of basic teachings we can turn to our own experience through our senses to find the Buddhist religion as a living path.

This book is an attempt to outline some important features of Buddhism prominent in the *Theravāda* tradition and to suggest how to find illustrations and timely lessons in our own surroundings. This is not a comprehensive introduction but rather a sheaf of sketches of life from a Buddhist perspective. With all our interests and energies, we remain limited, mortal beings, subject to many kinds of confusion and loss, and we need to find landmarks, certainties, reliable truths in order to direct ourselves skillfully. The essays that follow here deal with common problems and questions of the spiritual seeker. They are intended not only to present information but also to draw attention to the beauty and magnificence of the Buddha's message and to encourage contemplation and worthy effort.

The quotations from Pali scriptures are edited excerpts from translations published by the Buddhist Publication Society of Kandy, Sri Lanka, whose meritorious work over many years has made much vital wisdom available to students.

Throughout the book Pali technical terms are used rather than their Sanskrit equivalents.

Bhikkhu Nyanasobhano

1. *In the Wilderness*

🌿 Probably to most of us there have come exceptional, unworldly moments, like unsuspected deeps in a stream, when we fell through appearances—fell through ourselves—into an intuition of majesty and wonder. Perhaps we rounded a corner at sunset and saw the landscape charged with a rare light, or whirled away from company into a dark street where snow swooped down in a hush, or crossed a bridge, a field, a clearing in solemn pines, and experienced a mood half of pain and half of exaltation that briefly dissolved mundane thoughts. At such times we stretched our limits and reached—for what? A flock of questions and longings scattered like birds into the distance, leaving us waiting for some radiance to come back on the wind.

We are not the first to have felt like this. Countless generations have mused over such passing inspirations, hoping to see truth blaze up before the ordinary dullness closed in again. Unlike the coarse pangs that have briefly thrilled us, these are ambiguous meteors in the sky of the mind that hint—if we can find words for it—that what we have called life is a narrow and shabby thing and that a grander reality forever escapes us.

We are too busy to attend long to such glimpses, being occupied by a host of wants, fantasies, worries, and obsessions of all kinds. We are busy; we have things to *do*. Nobody knows quite why, but nearly everybody accepts that it is important and imperative to keep running, keep obeying the unseen spur of desire. There is education to be digested, wealth and love to be chased down, family to be built, projects to be carried out, achievements to be registered on plaques, and fun—oh, much fun—to be crammed into our senses. And one thing more: pain to be avoided. It would seem that because we have fingers we must fiddle in every piece of business within reach, because we have legs we must use them for bounding after entertainment, because we have a brain we must keep it hotly cranking to suppress any outbreak of uncertainty.

Everybody pretends to despise accumulation of things, but everybody accumulates. It is simply a practical requirement, we tell ourselves, a necessity for realizing the good life of abundance and self-fulfillment, and we must stay busy, absorbed, intense—even as stray moments of wonder glimmer like meteors overhead. When we leave our school years behind and venture bravely into what we think to be adulthood, we resolve with the confidence of youth that, unlike the sorry generations before us, we will not submit to the restraints of society but will cut our own splendid path through the world. How dispiriting, then, to discover in a few years that, far from constricting us, society has yielded us enormous scope, an unfenced range in which to run ourselves to death. Left to our own devices, we have been bullied by them and called in a score of others to our aid, until we are fairly reeling from one burdensome privilege to another. So many demands on our time! So many demands welling up—from where? Summer with its fragrances, winter with its gales—but through all seasons a subtle strain persists. At night, as we stare at the bedroom ceiling, thoughts troop through our minds like endless files of petitioners, laying on us this debt, that duty, this fear, that necessity, until we sleep, and wake again, eternally servants to busyness. How did we ever fall to this bondage?

In gloom or listlessness we ask ourselves what the purpose of all of this is. But when we ask without force at a low time the question dies away, rhetorical and fruitless. The best time to ask ourselves what is really significant and valuable in our experience is when we have disciplined our minds to contemplate or when we have momentarily drifted out of fierce currents—especially in those odd moments of spiritual attention: when the singing of insects strangely eases the heart, or the dripping in wet woods points to a greater stillness, or a silver wave blows through grass like memory through time. Then we might profitably ask ourselves, and look alertly for an answer.

In cold materialistic terms no earthly success lasts for long. Pile up an empire, if you will, but soon enough others will possess your mansions and erase your name. Lie low and tend your roses—still oblivion will find you out. Some tears are dropped, if you are lucky, and then you are forgotten, and whatever reverence, fear, or love you excited cools. So it has been and will be. The great and the humble totter down the same solitary, mortal track. But if this is all that can be said about the human career, shall we plunge at once into the hot ferment of the world, into noise and opinion and urgent competition? If destruction awaits us, shall we make haste to gulp down all the enjoyment we can? Indeed, we are powerfully drawn toward such desperate conclusions, not trusting ourselves to climb toward peace and equanimity, which we only glimpse and do not understand. We suspect that present entertainments will disappoint us, but rather than set out, of our own will, on a lonely, windy way, we burrow deeper into distractions. So we get busy and so we get more desperate.

But the stuff of the world will not hold together for long. In our best times we realize that and surge briefly above grubby habit, feeling a curious detachment and a yearning for something nobler. How can we be happy, and how can we get free, and might they ultimately be the same thing? If all that we might *acquire* is temporary, as it appears to be, might not deliverance lie in an entirely new direction? Why should the thought of deliverance even arise in this universe of endless diversions? Out of our musing such questions take shape, then melt away when our attention fails or anxiety heats up again. No time to think, so much to do!—here in our sphere of faulty but indispensable delights.

But why should our delights be indispensable? What drives us from one dissatisfaction to another? Too often we have found the delectable and the poisonous mingled in the same cup. Human life gets sorely entangled with pleasure and pain, joy and grief, hope and despair, and we cannot, for all our skill and gasping intensity, pick out just the good parts. The weather shifts; a smiling moment leads in its grim successor; we get fooled; we get hurt. Still we cannot let go of sharp wanting, and still we go on bleeding out our strength and crying secret tears, and still, oblivious to our desperation, the wild stream of circumstance twists and flows. Things, we observe forlornly, keep changing.

Nevertheless, in the midst of habit, a healthy doubt will keep returning to serious persons—a radical doubt that probes the foundation of the universe and the foundation of the mind itself. Things indeed keep changing. Let us knock down our philosophy to this block and build anew. We do right to doubt as long as doubt sets us to contemplation with eager minds, acknowledging our fundamental ignorance amid lapsing appearances. Things change and we change. What anchor, then, could we hold onto? Where is the *end* of doubt, where is the ultimate harbor to which we should steer? And who exactly are *we* who wish for peace? Too long we have been numbly content, or resigned, to let these questions pass, while still thinking ourselves rational and intelligent. An honest appraisal—an honest doubt—will not suffer such negligence, but will force us to lay open old assumptions, especially the great taken-for-granted belief that "I" am an inviolable, indivisible "self" proceeding through a substantial world toward permanent well-being and happiness. If this belief is true, then why should doubt occur at all? Why should fear? Why should we experience those glancing moments of awe? Why do melancholy and regret so ravage us beneath our public cheer?

Keen questioning, probing through the jungle of our days, seems to open the way only to a deeper solitude, until in the little free space we have made we find, if we read the signs, that we are not the first to have ventured so far, and that a path leads onward from this spot. The name of the path is *Dhamma*, and it has been here all along, though it only becomes known to the world when a Buddha rediscovers it and points it out.

In our unhappy ignorance we might think that only by spurning all forms of belief could we have a chance of uncovering truth or escaping error, but by doing so we would distort wise caution to willful delusion. A critical attitude of mind should never prevent us from acting when acting is called for, as it certainly is when a path appears in the baneful wilderness. Which shall it be—off again through the thorny waste, or onward along the promising track?

The Pali word "Dhamma" (*Dharma* in Sanskrit) means true nature, the fundamental, liberating facts of reality, and the course of practice that leads to deliverance from all suffering. The Buddha, the Enlightened One, was the sage Siddhattha Gotama, who by his own efforts penetrated the ultimate mysteries of existence and then traveled about India, teaching the Dhamma for the welfare of men and women and all living beings. The Buddha referred to himself as a *Tathāgata*, which means "thus gone" or "thus come"—attained to supreme wisdom and liberation. He was one who had fully understood the world and transcended it. He was not a god or a supernatural being but a man who fulfilled the highest possibility of mankind, who broke through ignorance into perfection with his realization of this best of all paths.

The Dhamma as taught by the Buddha is at once a transcendent path and a practical one, the experience of which refutes the popular belief that higher consciousness must somehow require the surrender of common sense. Doubters and wanderers in search of certainty have often felt compelled to choose between ungoverned emotion and lifeless intellect, and thus have spiraled away on one wing with neither earth nor heaven steady in view. But the path of Dhamma is a way without extremes. The rational faculty, so highly admired in this scientific age, has its essential place, as it directs and supervises human effort with an understanding of how the world works and what promotes welfare and prosperity. It focuses the higher, intuitive faculty, which strikes directly into reality beyond conceptual categories and lifts the mind to states of balance and clarity infinitely removed from ignorant passion.

The Dhamma beautifully encompasses the twin problems of thoughtful people: how to get along serenely day to day in the toils of the world, and how to overcome the world and all its suffering forever. Too often we think these goals incompatible, but the Buddha shows them as complementary and mutually strengthening. The higher life, that abiding in holiness we somehow feel to be possible, needs as its basis a daily life nobly conducted, a porch well swept, a heart made tranquil; and the efforts to maintain a peaceful and comfortable family or to follow a satisfying professional career require for their success a communion with what is loftier and a faith in the interrelationship of actions. The religious person gazes upon streaking meteors, and waters his garden with conviction. He knows where he stands; he senses subtle currents; he acts according to Dhamma. Distress and alienation come about from not knowing and appreciating the vital interplay between the holy and the mundane, and this the Dhamma can remedy by making clear the consequences of thoughts, words, and deeds, and the benefits of understanding the processes of nature. Who would have supposed that worldly aggravations could be lessened by contemplating raindrops on a railing? Or that the most refined spiritual practices could be impeded or advanced by how attentively we wash the breakfast dishes? But connections exist. The Dhamma surprises its followers with new avenues of understanding— not of remote, esoteric matters, but of the factual business of living and becoming wiser and happier than we are now.

The Buddha understood that men and women are not, by and large, wise or truly happy, nor can they become so in the pursuit of seeming pleasure. His own strenuous search had led him to the solution of the problem in the Four Noble Truths—four profound, comprehensive facts or summations of existence. The first of these is the truth of suffering or *dukkha*. Birth, he saw, is suffering; likewise old age, death, sorrow, lamentation, pain, grief, despair, association with the undesired, separation from the desired, not getting what one wants, and even the basic, intertwined, material and mental components of a person. To the Buddha, what mattered above all else was putting an end to this oppressive suffering, this endlessly recurrent unsatisfactoriness, this *dukkha*. Here he moved counter to other thinkers who, in varying degrees of refinement, conceive of getting something *more*—pleasure, beauty, power, delight, knowledge—as compensation or counterbalance for the eternally unremedied suffering. He recognized the futility of piling more experience, be it ever so enchanting, on top of a crumbling base, and instead pressed on toward total freedom from all that was painful and obstructive, from the whole mass of repetitious misery. This *dukkha* was a pervasive condition that could not simply be smoothed out or hidden. But it could be destroyed.

The Buddha realized that pain, grief, woe, and suffering have their source and origin in craving (*taṇhā*). This is the second noble truth. This craving is the primal thirst that goes forever unslaked, sucking up oceans of sensation but still breathing out flames of *dukkha*. It may be classified into three forms: sensual craving, craving for existence, and craving for nonexistence. As long as craving rages unchecked, suffering will follow it, day to day and life to life, buffeting and searing the mind, which in its ignorance craves even more, throws up more passion, more straw for the flames—and round and round it goes. Having felt this, one feels that; having become this, one becomes that—and on and on but nowhere an end. When *this* arises *that* arises, then again something else. Events occur in a continuous, conditioned stream, sometimes pleasant, sometimes unpleasant, sometimes neutral, but always unsettled, flawed, twitching with unrest—as in a frantic costume ball in which the masks keep changing. Craving needles the mind, and the arm stretches out for objects. Then there is frustration, grasping, taking hold. Then, after the flicker of pleasure: disappointment, anxiety, loss, regret, and puzzlement. Then craving, unsated, flares again. Things are not reliable—they change; and the mind changes, too, trying on new masks over the same sad incomprehension.

The Buddhist answer to the problem of suffering is to break up and renounce this obsessive desire once and for all, rather than to keep chasing the phantoms of worldly delight. The third noble truth is the truth of the cessation of suffering. By completely abandoning and forsaking craving we can abolish suffering and achieve freedom. After all these years and aeons of incompleteness, we need a permanent happiness, not just fits of stimulation, so we must strip away decoration and seek foundations. We yearn for security, so we must not addict ourselves to the nonsecure. In the smoking landscape of desire and loss, what will protect us? Liberation must be the goal, not a softer bed in the prison of craving. Therefore the Buddha's teaching is an instruction in getting free of craving. That done, everything is done. When *this* ceases *that* ceases. When ignorance is destroyed and craving withers away, greed, hatred, and delusion cannot come to be, and suffering, cut off at the roots, must expire and disappear. Then there can no longer be any mental affliction, or spiritual uncertainty, or confusion. The perfected one sees the universe just as it is, and experiences what the Buddha called "that unshakable deliverance of the heart."

The fourth noble truth discovered by the Buddha is the practical way to this deliverance, the comprehensive program for release from suffering. This is the Noble Eightfold Path, which consists of right view, right intention, right speech, right action, right livelihood, right effort, right mindfulness, and right concentration. These eight factors are not stages or steps to be perfected one after another but rather eight aspects of training to be developed together.

Right view is proper understanding of suffering as the central fact of sentient existence, and understanding also of suffering's origin, its end, and the way to that end. Mundane right view is recognition of the power of good or bad deeds to bring about benefit or suffering for the doer of the deeds. Higher right view is the understanding and the eventual penetration of the Four Noble Truths themselves, which result in enlightenment.

Right intention is intention characterized by renunciation or non-greed, absence of ill will, and harmlessness.

Right speech is abstention from false speech, slanderous speech, harsh or abusive speech, and senseless, useless talk; or in positive terms, speech that is true, reliable, discreet, polite, reasonable, and pleasing to hear.

Right action is abstention from killing, stealing, and sexual misconduct.

Right livelihood is the avoidance of dishonest or harmful occupations and the getting of a living through fair, moral occupations.

Right effort is the conscious, energetic effort to avoid unwholesome states that have not yet arisen, to overcome unwholesome states that have already arisen, to develop wholesome states that have not yet arisen, and to keep up wholesome states that have already arisen.

Right mindfulness is attentive observation of all aspects of mind and body so as to know, clearly and simply and without attachment, what is happening at any moment.

Right concentration is the wholesome concentration of the mind on an object so as to attain powerful clarity and profound tranquility.

The Buddha taught on these subjects long and thoroughly, knowing them to be supremely useful, so it is worth our while to pay heed and use his wise instruction to support our aspirations. In reaching for the highest we can by no means neglect our duties in rough or tedious life here and now—and indeed, here and now are exactly where we want relief and happiness. Like lamps in every room of a house, the eight factors of the Noble Eightfold Path reveal with a smoke-free light all the powers we wield for our own good and the good of others, showing us that by skillful management of such plain matters as speaking, working, and paying attention we can dispel sorrow, purify our understanding, and bring satisfaction and meaning to our labors. Deliverance of the heart does not come about through indulgence in incoherent states of mind, or through reliance on rituals, or through intellectual cleverness, or through stolid patience alone. We can achieve deliverance by consciously cutting through the bonds we have tied around ourselves, by resisting and ultimately destroying greed, hatred, and delusion, by making a final end of ignorant craving. The Noble Eightfold Path is the necessary means for accomplishing this, and if we keep to it, gradually refining our aim, it will guide us and console us and nourish us with wisdom.

Such is the rational, realistic outlook of Buddhism—no dreamy mysticism here. No feverish materialism, either, cackling over piles of crumbs. The Buddhist raises his or her eyes to the sky, not in expectation of showers of gold or accidental blessings, but in search of bare truth, weather signs, a higher way of striving, patterns to arouse the mind. However sharp the hunger, however keen the pain, nobody gets out of the jungle of troubles without making a sustained, personal effort. On all sides despondent multitudes shuffle, some longing for good luck, some expecting the genii of science, industry, or art to clear the way, to stop the pain. The Buddhist goes by way of Dhamma—the middle way—and does the walking alone, stumbles and gets up again, picks off the thorns, gets in the open and stays there with determined effort—no slave to false hope, no listless idler, and yet no superman: just a thinking being who has become convinced that the fearful storms of the universe are born in and burst out of his own heart and that nobody can quell them but him.

The negligent see their days and seasons as the tricky dice of fate, to be sweated over and implored. The attentive do not rely on uncontrollable twists of events but make their quiet progress by the lamps of nature—for Dhamma is nature rightly examined and rightly known. A resolute attention to the course of things, to the laws that shape the course, strikes off the sparks of insight that light our darkness. Provocative moments come—meteors lovely in their glittering flight—and pass away again. May that light, that trill of bird song, that sweet wind not vibrate in our thought for nothing but give rise to a brave will in us. How far then might we—bruised and baffled in the wilderness—journey by this old and beautiful wisdom? The Buddha, lost in history, beyond history, majestic, immovable, and gently smiling, speaks of suffering and the end of suffering. The learning and the going must be our tasks. How can we know if we have the strength? Let us step forward and see. The Buddha points, and as we turn to look the breezes of spring rush past us, bound for far places. A gate swings open and the path lies fair.

2. Meditation in the Light of Day

🍃 For those who have not been brought up in Buddhist families the practice of meditation has often served as the entrance to the Buddhist religion. The relentless tension, materialism, and banality of modern society drive thoughtful people to seek an escape to some dearly imagined peace or balance, or at least a means of neutralizing the daily attack on the senses. Even those accustomed to the battering stimuli of urban or suburban hustle may turn curious and wistful when they hear the word "meditation." It raises visions, or feelings, or delicate longings for an ideal never wholly lost to thinking beings: a state of unassailable peace and poise, a refuge of wisdom. Most people never get beyond vague hankering and never control their agitation long enough to investigate systematically, but some find their way to some sort of practice that they hope will give them access to a finer reality or to a finer way of dealing with present circumstances.

Often Buddhist meditation is misunderstood, even by devoted adherents, as a stylized, esoteric exercise requiring special scenic preparations and uninterrupted silence, preferably in a place distinct from the ordinary. Take away gongs, candles, incense, and cushions, and snap on the lights or raise the window shade—and some practitioners may get disturbed and think that meditation is no longer possible or has been robbed of necessary atmosphere. But such a view is as mistaken as that of non-meditators who dismiss meditation as self-indulgent nonsense.

To advance from mere posing into real practicing—into real movement on the Noble Eightfold Path—we need first to come to a sound understanding of what meditation really means and what purpose it serves in Buddhism. The important Pali word which could be translated as "meditation" is *bhāvanā*. But *bhāvanā* means a great deal more than formal sitting. It means mental development, the gradual disciplining of a rough, uneven mind to make it fit for work. The mind is, among other things, a tool for uncovering truth and rooting out sorrow, one easily dulled by misuse. *Bhāvanā* protects and sharpens this tool so that it will become serviceable for hard use and will not fly apart when brought to bear on the problems, passions, and complexities of life.

In the widest sense, then, mental development is a skillful, systematic effort to improve and purify one's mind and consequently one's behavior; it includes, as one part, the formal sitting discipline most people think of as meditation. Mental development can indeed be the work of the whole of one's life, directed along the Noble Eightfold Path. But in expanding the definition of mental development to its fullest extent, one must be careful not to dilute it and lose the sense of urgency and the awareness that, for the Buddhist, there is always something to be *done*, and done with care and due reflection.

In technical terms, there are two main branches of Buddhist meditation: *samatha-bhāvanā* and *vipassanā-bhāvanā*. The first refers to a system of training the mind to attain states of extraordinary tranquility and concentration. With its emphasis on strictly limiting attention to a single object and rigorously excluding other phenomena until exalted levels of contemplation are achieved, *samatha-bhāvanā* has much in common with practices in other religions, though its ultimate purpose is to prepare the mind for the uniquely Buddhist insight into suffering and the way to the end of suffering.

Samatha practice is characterized by the exercise and development of concentration, which calms the mind, suppresses mental impurities or defilements, wards off distractions, and bestows joy, steadiness, and peace on the practitioner. In trying to build such potent concentration, Buddhists have traditionally applied themselves to any of forty classical meditation subjects. These range over all of ordinary experience and beyond to highly abstract fields of contemplation. The ancient list (elaborated in detail in Buddhist literature) consists of the following: ten representations or symbols of earth, water, fire, wind, blue color, yellow color, red color, white color, light, and limited space; ten stages of bodily decay; ten recollections—of the Buddha, his teaching (the Dhamma), the community of noble disciples, morality, generosity, heavenly beings, death, the body, in-and-out breathing, and peace; four "divine abodes"—loving kindness, compassion, sympathetic joy, and equanimity; four immaterial spheres—boundless space, boundless consciousness, nothingness, and neither-perception-nor-nonperception; perception of loathsomeness of food; and analysis of the basic physical elements.

As evident even in outline form, *samatha* practice offers a wealth of themes and approaches for meditation. No one doing this practice, however, is expected to master or even to undertake all of them. The character or circumstances of individual practitioners might call for different kinds of practice at different times, and an experienced teacher might prescribe certain subjects to overcome particular problems or to develop needed virtue or understanding. But to one degree or another, all the techniques of *samatha* lead toward mental balance, tranquility, and concentration, even up to the exalted states called *jhānas*. Many people suffer from scattered minds, nervousness, fear, and distraction, so *samatha* by its calming action may give profound relief and lead to great strength and clarity of mind. However, it needs for its fullest development periods of seclusion and conditions of quiet that are hard to come by in the modern world. Also, *samatha* meditation, which produces only temporary calm and suppression of harmful mental factors, cannot by itself achieve the very highest goal—enlightenment. For that the spiritual pilgrim must turn sooner or later to *vipassanā-bhāvanā*, or insight meditation.

In the *Theravāda* or "doctrine of the elders," this insight means direct experience of existence as (1) impermanent (*anicca*), (2) suffering or unsatisfactory (*dukkha*), and (3) impersonal or devoid of self (*anattā*). While meditators can and should prepare themselves, and later enlarge their understanding, with intellectual knowledge of these three characteristics of existence, only direct confrontation with them can loosen the ancient logjam of ignorance. In fact, the world swarms with evidence of the three characteristics, yet within the haze of delusion we repeatedly mistake fantasy for reality.

Thus, some kind of systematic mental discipline to remove delusion is necessary. *Vipassanā* meditation may in fact employ some of the same subjects as *samatha* meditation, though its emphasis is less on intensifying concentration and more on detecting and comprehending the underlying truths of existence. In order to put an end to suffering we must conquer and eliminate craving—not only suppress it for a time, not only enjoy temporary attainments—and to make this conquest we must win our way to an unobstructed vision of who we are and where we stand.

Enlightenment—that magnificent escape from anguish and ignorance—never happens by accident. It results from the brave and sometimes lonely battle of one person against his own weaknesses—the earnest, persevering effort to put aside what is not wholesome and to make clear what is not yet clear. Even with the finest intentions, nobody is going to realize the full benefits of *vipassanā* meditation by fiddling randomly with theories or dabbling in mental exercises or rolling along the easiest way. We cannot hope to be saved from present dread and future misery without exertion, without committing our full attention, and we cannot expect to find supermundane knowledge in some book or class or ceremony. The active man or woman, who wishes to take charge of his or her destiny, should practice insight meditation with determination and with a heart fortified with reverence for the ideal of enlightenment.

Suppose someone sees or claims to see impermanence, suffering, and nonself *without* meditating—just after scriptural study or logical consideration. Would this qualify as insight? What is the special value of personal experience? Indeed, students of Buddhism might stop short or bog down in the notion that through their acquaintance with written doctrine they have absorbed the basic meaning of the Dhamma and need not actually subject themselves to what they fear would be a trying, disagreeable discipline. Regardless of the extent of their intellectual knowledge, that would be a regrettable mistake. It is a fundamental teaching in Buddhism that craving is the source of suffering and that to eliminate suffering one must completely eradicate craving. As anyone knows who has investigated even a little, getting rid of craving is no simple matter of decision, no intellectual exercise. One might admit rationally and intellectually that craving harms one's well-being in countless ways, yet be quite unable, when put to the test, to remove even the smallest scrap of it. A deeper motivation is called for.

This motivation is found in the understanding of where craving itself comes from. Fundamentally, craving arises from and is inseparable from ignorance about the nature of reality. Not understanding that all the phenomena of the dazzling world are supported by impermanent conditions and hence ultimately unreliable and unsatisfactory, we give way to superficial attractions; we set loose the urgent, unresting tides of craving. As long as this primal condition of ignorance persists, so will craving and so will suffering. This ignorance is not a simple intellectual lack, an absence of succinct information, but a deep spiritual destitution, which can only be remedied by direct, experiential understanding.

In dealing with the basic problem of craving, *vipassanā* meditation has a powerful, educational effect, because it presents reality to the mind immediately, with undeniable force, in such a way as to undermine the ancient fortress of ignorance. Suppose, for example, that a worried miser carries everywhere with him a bag of money, nervously guarding it, refusing to open it and spend any of it; and then someone comes and persuades him to open the bag to the light of day, revealing that it now holds nothing but chewed paper and a dead rat. Would not the owner at once drop the bag in disgust? No further debate is necessary—he sees and he lets go. *Vipassanā* meditation works in a similar way, exposing our deepest beliefs to light and naturally causing us to let go of the false ones.

While we are still oppressed by ignorance and consequently subjected to ever-renewed craving and suffering, we do not see clearly; we do not know things in their real nature. We look out at the world and see appealing, attractive, lasting things that we might possess; and without instruction to the contrary we readily set out in pursuit of them and, in due course, begin to suffer from the mischance, frustration, and chagrin that seem to be the woeful fate of all humanity. "Why such endless trouble?" we wonder. "What are we doing wrong?" Our mistake, it happens, is not so much in our bad luck or unskillful reaching as in our fundamental misperception of all those sparkling prizes. If they are *not* after all substantial things, and if we ourselves are not substantial egos, it stands to reason that our efforts have been misdirected to begin with, and that we must relearn the features of this country in which our birth has landed us. *Vipassanā* meditation is a method for this relearning. If we restrain our senses and observe carefully it becomes possible to cut through delusion and acquire accurate information about the universe, which we can then use to act intelligently. The grasping, agonizing phantom of self needs for its continuation (and the continuation of suffering) the delusion that the universe is stable, stocked with reliable pleasures, and peopled with enduring egos; thus, insight into the universal characteristics of impermanence, suffering, and impersonality comes as a salutary surprise.

Except in the remarkable cases of persons with much built-up virtue and wisdom, whose minds are prepared for a huge leap, insight grows gradually and unpredictably. As a skillful disciple meditates and begins to see everywhere an overwhelming impermanence—a constant rise and fall of phenomena—confidence in the power of beauty, wealth, and talent diminishes. As he or she begins to see pervasive suffering or unsatisfactoriness—the inherent flaws in all compounded, impermanent things—the idea of freedom rises in opposition to infatuation with empty pleasures. As the third characteristic of existence, nonself or impersonality, grows clearer, pride and self-satisfaction become increasingly absurd. In such a universe, what is there to clutch? At the end of training, at the last step of enlightenment, seeing directly, the noble person gives up all craving, and release becomes boundless. No need to speculate, no need to ponder—wisdom like a lightning bolt knocks down the confining walls.

To be effective in revealing truth, meditation or *bhāvanā* must include mindfulness (*sati*). Mindfulness means pure attentiveness, an alert, impartial function of mind that simply notes whatever appears by way of the senses of sight, hearing, smell, taste, touch, and mind itself. Mindfulness does not cogitate, judge, or interpret; it only observes, neutrally and without commentary, the actual character of an object or phenomenon. Despite its quiet, unglamorous nature, mindfulness occupies an essential position in the practice of meditation, and meditation masters, beginning with the Buddha himself, have extolled it as the unsurpassed means of penetrating reality.

Advanced minds perceive worth where others notice nothing special at all. Even eager new meditators may be disappointed at the emphasis placed on such a seemingly humdrum virtue as mindfulness if they have been anticipating oracular wonders and mystical thrills. Mindfulness, far from being an automatic, minor accomplishment of a meditator, is a vital force that, when properly established and applied, does exactly what most benefits seekers of liberation: it reveals things as they actually exist. Normally, according to Buddhist teaching, we see wrongly and incompletely, through a cloud of prejudice. In the process of perception, immediately after a phenomenon makes itself known through one of the six "doors" of eye, ear, nose, tongue, body, or mind, it becomes contaminated, so to speak, by reflexive liking or disliking, emotions, opinions, imagination, and so on. While we think ourselves autonomous and discriminating, we remain in thrall to mental custom, and with our perceptions skewed we cannot manage our lives with consistent skill. Mindfulness combats this custom. It filters out delusive impurities until the stream of experience runs purer, and the chronic sickness of confusion begins to subside.

The very plainness of mindfulness makes it useful everywhere, not just in sitting meditation but in daily life as well. A form of practice that would result in sensory excitement or unconsciousness to external events would not be suited to someone who has to dodge through dangerous automobile traffic every morning or supervise boisterous children or coordinate the many duties of work and home, but mindfulness established in the present moment eases the performance of these and all mental or physical tasks by bringing forward the essential facts without intellectual or emotional fanfare. Mindfulness serves like a skillful scout reporting to his commander: "This is happening; that is not happening; such-and-such has appeared; such-and-such has disappeared." The practitioner uses mindfulness to obtain clear information about the processes of body and mind and hence to deal judiciously and coolly with sensory experience, whether sitting quietly at home with no disturbance but the ticking of a clock or rushing down the highway among a thousand cars.

We might wonder, "How can I find time to practice meditation or mental development when I'm so *busy*, when a million things are going on at once?" But insight meditation is not an extra duty to be piled on top of our already overburdened minds, but rather a way of looking more clearly at what is actually happening. A practitioner of *vipassanā*, trying to cope better with this present state of existence as well as to attain ultimate liberation, trains himself or herself to rouse and employ mindfulness in all situations, to perceive simply what is there, to note calmly and objectively the rising and the passing away of phenomena, specifically with regard to (1) the physical body; (2) pleasant, unpleasant, and neutral feelings; (3) mind or consciousness; and (4) mental objects. The Buddha pointed out these four bases of understanding or foundations of mindfulness as supremely important:

> *This path, namely the Four Foundations of Mindfulness, is a path that goes in one way only: to the purification of creatures, to the surmounting of sorrow and lamentation, to the disappearance of pain and grief, to the attainment of the true goal, to the realization of Nibbāna [deliverance].*
> (Saṃyutta Nikāya XLVII, 18, 43)

Body, feelings, mind, and mental objects are always present, always available for inspection, so meditation can proceed whenever we set mindfulness to work on them. Mindfulness breaks down experience from great choking lumps to manageable bits. What we take to be solid objects and cohesive events turn out, under the light of mindfulness, to be dependent compounds of changing phenomena, all without intrinsic essence or stability. A great many problems and misfortunes, therefore, may be alleviated by quietly paying attention to the elements that make them up. When we have to undergo a difficult interview or face criticism, for example, we can use mindfulness by mentally noting the actual phenomenon of hearing—just the neutral recognition of bare events—thereby calming our usual, personal reaction to angry or abusive speech. Certainly we continue to understand what is being said (and understand better the calmer we are), but it is after all, as mindfulness discloses, just sound, just impermanent physical energy striking our sensory organs. When we are worried, harried, and overworked, mindfulness cuts out extraneous flutter and seeks the chief theme, the important item in any situation, much as in a crisis a talented manager might walk into a room full of screeching subordinates and single out the one who can give a coherent account of the problem.

Insight meditation has nothing to do with sluggish, self-absorbed fantasy, but goes with reason, clear comprehension, and practical wisdom. We need not soar off to the stars for fruitful truths. Impermanence, unsatisfactoriness, and impersonality characterize all aspects of conditioned existence and remain always accessible to meditators, whether they are sitting motionless in a temple or jouncing along in a city bus.

The effort to see clearly what is happening can and should continue in all circumstances. There is no time when mindfulness is not helpful, when it does not add at least a little brightness to our understanding. At work or amid the appointments of the day we might not have a silent hour at our disposal, but as we sit or walk or eat, the world goes on displaying itself to our senses, so we have only to focus to note what we usually ignore. When we walk across a room we can pay attention to the actual process of walking. When we touch and lift objects we receive sensory information about pressure, temperature, and motion that can be noted with a little effort. Drinking a cup of tea, we get sensations of heat, smell, and taste, of the touch of cup against lip, of the muscular motions of drinking. No need to *comment* on these; mindfulness merely notices, holding on to nothing. In moving and in sitting still the body furnishes a host of events, processes, twinges, discomforts, tics, etc. Likewise the mind entertains countless ideas and perceptions. They all come and go, come and go—and the consistent, moment by moment observation of these is meditation. When we have complicated or demanding work to do such an observant attitude does not slow us down at all; on the contrary, it lubricates the machinery of thought and speeds the job. Within the tumult of sense impression it opens a space of calm and clarity. The development of insight is the widening and deepening of this space.

Formal sitting and walking meditation also have an important function in the Buddhist system. Nearly everyone suffers from physical and mental distractions that bat the mind around like a bouncing ball, so teachers throughout the ages have set up frameworks of practice with specific exercises to perform. Mostly these exercises stay simple, as insight meditation is not concerned with the construction of grand mental edifices, the purpose being rather to observe, more and more acutely, how the universe actually operates.

In one style of sitting meditation, for example, one simply sits quietly and attempts to direct mindfulness to the objects that present themselves. One focuses on a main object, such as the rising and falling of the abdomen or the touch of breath going in and out the nose, and mentally registers the fact of rising and falling, or in and out. No attempt is made to control or alter the primary object. One sets aside the habitual commentary of the mind and the urge to do things, and tries just to observe the object, to see it exactly as it is. When other sense objects interrupt concentration, as they inevitably do, one shifts the focus of mindfulness temporarily and simply notices the experience of hearing or smelling or pain or whatever it is. When attention wanders, one clearly registers the fact of wandering or thinking, treating thoughts in the same impersonal, detached way as other objects. The immediate purpose here is not to control mind and body but just to *know* them as they are, as they change, and thereby to prune away some part of the thickets of ignorance.

In formal walking meditation the procedure differs only in that the moving of the foot becomes the main object of awareness. One walks back and forth slowly in a room or on a path, paying attention to the different phases of the walking movement, according to the instructions of the teacher. In stopping, standing, and turning, or in sitting or in lying down—in fact, in all postures—the meditator attends mindfully to the immediate object, trying to keep attention focused on it with steady concentration, but not worrying when distractions occur. What is important is to stay mindful and awake—not negligent or infatuated—in the present moment, alert to the changing stream of sense impressions.

One uses a principal meditation object as a reference point or focus of concentration, not as a charm to cling to. There is nothing special in the rising and falling of the abdomen or in the motion of the foot; these are merely convenient, present phenomena that have the nature to change and hence afford the meditator opportunities to see things in their fundamental nature. Just as in a dark room a flashlight will light up whatever object it is pointed at—the beam sweeping easily over rough and smooth, beautiful and ugly—so mindfulness lights up the crowding, jostling factors of mind and body. Understanding and practicing in this way, without strain or passion, one finds no limit at all to the field of meditation.

But to learn to practice meditation coolly and correctly requires study. It is not a matter for casual improvisation. There are many techniques, which should not be carelessly mixed. Students can get a start by reading books by reputable meditation teachers, but it is highly desirable to seek explicit training in technique in order to avoid straying down fruitless paths and wasting time and energy. One needs, moreover, to consult with an experienced person, to ask questions and have them answered, to observe and discuss problems.

Formal sitting or walking practice should not be thought of as a duty that, if carried out for a set period every day, fulfills the Buddhist obligation to develop the mind. We spend most of our days *informally* sitting or walking, and these activities need attention, too. All kinds of insight meditation are only means to the attainment of insight, and insight is the doorway to liberation, to the victory over sorrow and ignorance. Practicing meditation under the best conditions we can manage builds up our mindfulness and concentration so that we can go out into the difficult, chaotic scenes of daily existence strengthened and prepared not merely to survive but to push forward.

Perhaps we are glad to meditate in the fragrant serenity of a temple or in our own homes when noise and duties have abated, but when the period ends we might quickly (habit being so strong) switch back to our frantic mode of behavior. What meditation should do, and will do if well practiced, is to awaken the meditator to the seamless, elastic quality of mindful attention and the benefit of extending it to all hours and situations. The Buddha taught that the reach of mind can and must be immense:

> *I do not say that one can make an end of suffering without having reached the end of the world. And I further proclaim, friend, that in this very fathom-long body with its perceptions and thoughts, there is the world, the world's origin, the world's ending, and the path leading to the world's ending.*
>
> (Aṅguttara Nikāya IV, 45)

We will not be going anywhere in this life without body and mind. The Buddha, whose sovereign vision ranged over space and time, saw no place holier than this place, no time riper than this time—the here and now everlastingly full with truth. The water splashing over our hands in the washbasin, the pulse at our collar, the morning clamor of birds, the spiraling of snowflakes, the scent of pines, the ache of sudden memory, our breath fast or slow at any hour—are these not objects for meditation perpetually arising? The best meditation turns us with vigilant senses toward the play of existence to know it, from an independent stance, for what it is. If we run with shadows and phantoms we will fall exhausted before they do. Why not let them perform and stand our ground? Do we sigh for remote, holy places? Here are body and mind—wild and awesome territory to explore.

Multitudes sleep unquietly with dreams that cannot last, upheaval being the nature of body and mind and all compounded things. Meditation is not a sleep but a waking up to impermanence, suffering, and selflessness—to the nature of this wilderness our caravan traverses. We may sit with candles and bells in a beautiful hall, or stride city pavements with mindfulness in blazing daylight, or in any place keep the right time, the celestial time, in the lift and fall of our abdomens or the slow touch of air at our nostrils. Always the Dhamma requires of us activity, not passivity. Before the peace must come the search; before the calm must come the work. Whoever makes his way out of confusion does so by individual effort, sun up or sun down, in all weathers, contemplating dust and flowers and craving and fear, living at ease but not in trance, ungrasping and mindful, doing serenely what needs to be done, and discerning ahead through worldly smoke and rain a brightening landscape.

3. *Contemplation of a Once-Tree*

🍃 T HE SPECULATIVE OPINIONS of our fellow man have less to teach us than the plain facts of nature, the raw stuff that agitates our senses, but even the most delicate and beautiful sensation counts for nothing but stimulation if not accompanied by some knowledge of how to look, how to consider what appears. Words can give us sound ideas and point us out of doors or out of dreams toward what we might then notice and confirm for ourselves if we are alert enough. Fundamental truths of existence—which any thinking person will sooner or later wish to discover—spring up in the range of those whose senses are awake; and the Buddha's explanations of those truths—spoken from knowledge, not opinion—turn us anew to the concrete, the present, the actual, to the poor shrubs and rocks and unregarded flowers of the roadside. To practice Buddhism, then, we must become not simply theorists or dreamers but instructed travelers. Our pilgrimage need not be long, as the world counts distance, but epic nonetheless: over the barriers of habit, through the forests of doubt, beyond our circumscribed consciousness toward a freedom as yet scarcely imagined. We have, perhaps, puzzled our way through books and revolved the old mysteries in our heads and beaten back, for the moment, the petty obsessions that rule our days, and now it is time to take up eye, ear, nose, tongue, body, and mind and go out to see what we have missed.

So let us travel. Say it is winter. Any season will do, but let us now for the contemplation go deep into the abandoned park when the first snow seems near and the treetops creak and scrape together. We walk to jolt our muscles and our minds awake, sniffing and huffing, breaking sticks, leaning and stretching, glancing now at the tangles of briars, now at the broken nuts and pretty stones beneath us. West wind sizzles in the last tenacious oak leaves and pale sunlight momentarily sweeps the scene through a gap in the clouds. Away from us, wave on wave, cold brown hills roll into obscurity. The elements seem charged with a rich potential that tantalizes us as we climb the muddy, half-frozen path, as if some profound truth, some mighty verse, were about to boom in our ears.

Stop, listen, breathe. No words are heard, but we let our senses attend to what there is—rustle of twigs, unstable light, wind's blade on skin, smell of smoke from somewhere, thoughts as delicate and random as snowflakes. Can we make translation into words or, better, into the heart's understanding? So much experience blows through us and away. We would read appearance and know truth, but in this wilderness of impressions we hardly know where to turn.

Onward we ramble through the unpeopled woods, startling the squirrels, losing the path, forgetting it, winding between stumps and mossy boulders, plodding or teetering, swinging our arms for balance, following gullies and ridges as the whim takes us. We go on this way for a time, growing more reflective, then pause again to catch our breath. Our attention settles on a flat space before us where the downed leaves are graying to uniformity.

Here lies an old log, long fallen, long rotted, crumbling to the dark soil it came from. We stand here observing it, warmed by the walk, and think the obvious: "Ah, this old log, once a mighty tree, now a dead hulk. Such is the life of man. Let's move on." But wait, we have not begun to see. Any apt observer can pick a symbol out of nature and squeeze it for a quick sip of intellectual satisfaction, but today we are after stronger nutriment. What is unique about this old log? Nothing, it seems, and that is one characteristic that recommends it to our thought: it is nature taken unawares in its profoundly ordinary state that is nearly invisible to the eye on the lookout for marvels. It is a broken length of decomposing wood lying in the dirt half covered with drifted leaves. How did it come to fall here? Where is it going?

No stump is visible; the limbs are long gone, the bark vanished. Only this bulk or core of a once-tree yet remains. It was a tree, to be sure, unknown years ago, wind-wrecked or fallen from disease; now it lies and rots its long way to disappearance. *Anicca*, impermanent. It was a tree, of a certain species, and now we call it a rotten log. At what point did the one term fail and the other apply? From tree to log to mealy dust, there occurs a continual changing, a gliding of form into form that we follow imprecisely with language. And where, we might ask, where exactly in the life of men and women can we mark the movements from infancy to childhood to youth to maturity to old age? The stages we see and try to express in language do not exist outside of our imagination, because change never ceases, never pauses to draw a line and give us notice. We make our attempts with words to pin down experience long enough to grasp, but slippery moments slide by like water and the whole mass of life streams on sorrowfully toward the incomprehension of death.

The once-tree beneath us is something in its own right—a changing something. It is no more or less real than the living beech that now overshadows it. It no longer drops leaves but flakes and bits of altered wood, manifesting the incapacity and the passing of all forms. We are not sorry at its state—who could be sorry over a rotten log?— but we cannot help but sense the unease, the wreck therein. *Dukkha*, unsatisfactory. On and on goes the breaking up, a shifting from this to that, an irresistible transformation. The agitation is infinitesimal and galactic—the nature alike of leaves and logs and stars—and it reminds us uncomfortably of our own changing faces and temporary passions. Impersonal agents of nature have stripped the once-tree to essentials, and the essentials are not much. They are in fact provisional and empty themselves. What of our own "essentials"?

So damp, depleted, and colorless lies this log on the frigid ground that we would be quick to abandon it, but instead let us bend closer to examine its slow decay and study its landscape of cracks and fissures. Now we see it does have color—a reddish brown, mottled with gray-green lichens and moss. Flecks of its substance microscopically tremble in cobwebs. Showing a ruined grain and empty whorls where limbs were, it seems to hold together now only out of habit, and on the bottom it is already surrendering into the dirt. One blast of thunder should collapse it all to dust, but still it deteriorates, is eaten, sags slowly under the ancient sky. So slowly it changes, but yet it does change and cannot help it. The roots of beeches and oaks have got at it and are pulling its matter into new forms—obliterating distinctions and making it all ready to become leaf, root, and limb again in time. Had *we* the time, as the sky has, we might see the full circle. To what end runs this weary round?

We shake our heads, blow on our cold fingers, and are suddenly struck by the scars and creases on our hands. A human being puffs and hurries and mouths opinions, whereas a tree just vegetates in cycles. Are we the happier for our noise? Have we, for all our fidgeting fingers and nimble words, yet made of our humanity what it could be? Might we not seek out some pure peace, some joy, some gracious stillness, even in flying moments such as these? It is cold here. We hug ourselves, number our ribs, imagine the wind streaming through them. Who's here? Who's here but a bundle of processes? Matter and mind fired by unreasoned wanting drive the cycle of existence on and on without permanent satisfaction. We try to understand, but our thoughts skitter and vanish—who could trust them? The log holds no shape, contains no self, owns no identity. Is our claim to a self any stronger, or are we likewise *anattā*—selfless, a pattern of fluctuating conditions?

Our hearts thump evenly and, strangely, our somber reflections begin to give way to a sensation of ease in the unconcerned forest. For all the cold and emptiness here, nature gets along. Trees release a few late leaves high up that spin and flip and scatter through the branches. What might we release that would lighten us? Letting go of worthless encumbrances marks both the beginning and the end of the search— the beginning because we must cast off a certain quantity of habit and prejudice in order to start to work, and the end because, having seen through the endless cycle of existence, we might at last forsake, abandon, and let go of miserable craving altogether. We stand now merely at the beginning, perhaps, but in a promising place, an untamed border country congenial to pilgrims.

Wind gathers now and specks of snow fly like white insects about us while the mind withdraws to an unaccustomed vantage point and regards December impinging on the senses. We have long read into this universe what we would, but when the mind is calmed and attuned the influences of a deeper reality may make themselves felt—not as vulgar despair or excitement, but as balance, as beautiful evenness. Quick sunlight glances off us and off the swaying twigs and boughs of the forest, then disappears as the clouds close in. In all this immensity and motion our wisp of self becomes ridiculous. From the dwindling ruin at our feet to the blurs of gray above there is a show of forms, a flux of concepts, a gauze of moving patterns in which not even wood, earth, ice, or stone holds firm; and the whole ambiguous mass of world rollicks on impetuously. But now as we stand in watchfulness, poised and attentive, a quietness seems to come over nature even as it streams and blows, and our own inaudible breath flows in and out unclenched and easy. And now the impermanent moment passes and out of the stir of the heart a word builds and rises unspoken in our thought. The word is "Dhamma."

Here with ears freezing and toes growing numb, we remember that this wild net of universe that weighs us down might someday, with valiant effort, be thrown off and escaped. And even before complete deliverance the perplexed and querulous days we live could be brightened and enriched if we could keep the Dhamma foremost in mind. We must learn better how to look, how to regulate our senses, how to step across the once-tree into the center of things and not get lost. Instinct is the impulse, intelligence the walking stick, but the revealed Dhamma is the indispensable map, path, and guide.

The disintegrating log knows nothing of our thoughts or momentary presence; it flies on through a wilderness of change while we, alert to cold and wind and light, stand over it and feel our own unending transformations. Because we live, because our faculties are open, we may hope to break through form to peace. Seeing change, seeing unsatisfactoriness, seeing the self-less nature of existence, we might cease to grasp and then be freed. When these three facts are entirely seen and comprehended, craving will end, and with it suffering. Here in the forest the rise-and-fall of formations wonderfully continues. The pulpy wood of the log is flaked, split, pulverized, riddled by insects, worn down by time. Stoop and touch these relics—they break loose, they sprinkle on our fingers, nearly weightless, as if the memory or mere convention of wood were all that held them here. Might we not shatter the greater convention of our suffering?

Now the light shuts down, the cold starts us shivering, and it is time to leave. But we linger perhaps one last minute in this borderland, conscious of grand and quiet motions in nature all around. The brown hills stand out, inexplicably beautiful, against the vast gray sky. Now slowly and easily the wind curls and washes over the land, and another little sprinkle of snow comes down, and we wait in reverence as the snowflakes drift and fall—one, two, then three—three crystals on the senseless log.

4. Nothing Higher to Live For

🍃 IF IT IS POSSIBLE TO LIVE with a purpose, what should that purpose be? A purpose might be a guiding principle, a philosophy, or an ideal of sovereign importance that informs and directs our actions. To have one is to live seriously (though not necessarily wisely), following some track, seeking in the maze of the world a special goal or an end before which all the hubbub of vanity subsides. What is your purpose, friend, or what should it be?

Perhaps most of us do not come to a definite conclusion in the matter, but this does not mean we have no purpose, only that we do not recognize it or admit it or even choose it for ourselves. In the unhappiest case nature simply pulls us along in a witless meandering through the swamps of desire. If life means nothing then only pleasure, it seems, is worthwhile; or if life has meaning and we cannot get at it then still only enjoyment is worth chasing—such is the view of the hopeless. It slips into the mind by default when we hold no other, but we are reluctant to entertain it and will rather, if we think about it, take as our purpose support of family, creation of beauty, social charity, fame, self-expression, development of talent, and so on. But it might be fair to say that apart from these or beneath these, deep and urgent, a fundamental purpose of many of us is the search for love, especially romantic love.

This is often the floor to which people fall after the collapse of other dreams. It is held to be solid when nothing else is, and though it frequently gives way and lets them drop into a basement of despair, it still enjoys a reputation of dependability. No matter that this reputation is unreasonable—it still flourishes and will continue to flourish regardless of what is said in any book. Love, or possibly the myth of love, seems to offer an enchanted refuge for longing, dreaming humanity. What else makes our hearts beat so fast? What else makes us swoon so with feeling? What else renders us so intensely alive? The pursuit of love— the sublime, the nebulous, the consuming—remains sacred in a world that often despises the sacred. When the heroic and the transcendental are only memories, when our religious sentiment declines unnoticed into complacency and worldliness, when nobody believes there is a sky beyond the ceiling, then there seems no other escape from the prison of self-concern than the abandon of love. With a gray age of fatigue upon us, we love, or beg for love, or grieve for love. We have nothing higher to live for.

Indeed, many take it on faith that romantic love *is* the highest thing to live for. Popular literature, movies, television, and music tirelessly celebrate it as an enduring, accessible truth. Such love, giddily set free, silences reason, and this is part of its charm and power, because we obscurely want to be swept up and spirited out of our pedestrian selves. In the spiritual void of modern times the wanting of love becomes nearly indistinguishable from love itself. So powerful, so insistent is it that we seldom notice that contentment is rare and craving relentless. Love seems to consist mostly in unripened hope; it is an ache for a completion amid the incompleteness of the present. That we never seem to possess it in its imagined fullness does not deter us. We worry at our pain as if to convert it somehow into joy.

Practically no one questions the magnificence of romantic love— which is good enough reason to do a little poking around its pedestal. Who is completely satisfied with the romance in his or her life? Who has found the sublime rapture previously imagined? And if someone has actually found such a thing, does it last, or does it not rather change and subside in time? And if it subsides, if it turns merely ordinary, what becomes of one's purpose in life? If a purpose is achieved it is no longer a purpose; it can no longer guide or sustain. Does one sip of joy end thirst forever?

When we tire of coarse, material goals we might go looking for love instead of religious insight because love seems both more accessible and more urgent. Longing for intense and moving experience, we turn to the vision of the "lover," that source of joy and comfort who, we vaguely suppose, can be pursued, captured, and retained indefinitely. Love is its own justification, especially for the young who have no other inspiration and who readily leap into adventure. Careers and wealth and recreation are well and good—but where else is there such an avenue of transcendence? They do not reason but fall. Their elders *do* reason, obsessively, but fall all the same, thereby admitting that, with all their thought and theory and painful memory, when pressed or inspired they have at last nothing higher than love to live for.

This is not to say that such a surrender must always be bad, only that it happens out of instinct and uninformed desire. Love is sweet, and it is human nature to give way. It is no doubt an opportunity to reach at least a little way out of the shell of self-absorption. But why do we worship it with such desperation and why do we break off our search for fulfillment here? Perhaps it is because we see no superior wonders. Yet if love is the highest thing to live for then this is a hopeless universe, because, as we should understand in a tranquil and reflective hour, the arrows of passion not only thrill us but make us bleed.

So often we hear of violence, viciousness, jealousy, and wretchedness arising out of some sort of passionate attachment. Countless shocking incidents in human experience suggest that romantic love is not always a blessing. We might object that hate, not love, spawns such tragedies, but where has such hate come from if not from an attachment distorted or broken? We should know from experience and observation how easily what we call love can yield to bitterness, jealousy, and malice; and although we might wish to believe that this is not the fault of *love*, we ought to notice that where one passion appears another is likely to follow. Passions are unreliable, volatile, and dangerous, and can make no safe foundation for happiness.

Divorces, rivalries, quarrels, dissipation, violence, and other miseries great and small follow from passion, and yet passion is still, in the haze of public myth, admired as evidence of liveliness and vigor. Although we will admit that passion gone awry is dangerous, we are slow to realize that passion is by its nature *likely* to go awry. Romantic love is a chancy passion that may result in the opposite of what is hoped for. It may certainly have happy consequences, too—or else it would not have had so many votaries throughout history—but it comes always with liabilities and makes us more vulnerable both to our own weaknesses and to unpredictable fortune. Intense emotions have intense effects.

As most of the world counts the blessings of successful love (however defined) as worth the pain involved in its pursuit, we must at least learn to step lightly and with intelligence. We believe that mature love can enrich us and redeem us and call forth our pure energies, but we are reluctant to consider that when the lamp of love flickers out, as it tragically tends to do, we might lose our way in a fearful labyrinth of suffering. Granted that most people will not shun the pursuit of romance out of fear of unhappy consequences, what can be done at least to soften those consequences? If we really have nothing higher to live for, the lugubrious truth is that little can be done, given the unstable, conflicting nature of human affections. But if, before committing ourselves exclusively to the chase, we acquire faith in a superior, sustaining ideal, we can learn to act with more sense and less trouble.

The ideal that Buddhism teaches is called *Nibbāna* (*Nirvāṇa* in Sanskrit). This is absolute peace, the release from affliction, the ultimate liberation, the escape from the miseries of rebirth. While worldly joys are mutable and fleeting, *Nibbāna* is firm, sorrowless, and secure. While worldly pains are piercing, unpredictable, and recurrent, *Nibbāna* is altogether free from pain. It is the end of suffering, the vanishing of all greed, hatred, and delusion. It is the highest happiness, the incomparable emancipation. The Buddha himself applied many terms of praise to it while recognizing their essential inadequacy. *Nibbāna* cannot be encompassed by language or concept, but it can be realized, even in this present life, by one who makes the right efforts. This is an important point. *Nibbāna* is not something that happens because of luck or fate or any external agency; rather it is something that the ardently practicing individual person might achieve. The Buddha certainly never would have troubled himself to teach had he not understood that his own realization was not accidental but rightly won and that those who followed his instructions faithfully could win realization for themselves. That understanding, passed down, has supported the Buddhist religion to the present day. The diligent are not powerless, and the goal can be reached.

Still, knowing ourselves to be often lost in confusion and challenged by thorny troubles, we might regard *Nibbāna* as too remote to do us much good right now. We persist in imagining an unbridgeable chasm between saints and ordinary people like ourselves. We think practically everybody is like us, while maybe there are one or two genuine saints somewhere, who presumably were just born in that condition. Yet the condition of sentient beings is not, according to Buddhism, a fixed sentence to this or that level of wisdom and virtue. Beings live at various stages of development, and they do not stay forever in one place. They rise through their own good efforts and decline through their own negligence, in the endless action and reaction of intentional deeds and results of deeds.

The Buddha did not teach the Dhamma simply for the consolation of those already perfected; he taught it for the benefit of fallible people who were struggling to avoid pain, make sense of life, and gain real joy. To such people he gave the progressive training of giving, morality, and mental development. Why? Because for an attentive person improvement is always possible, and because the human alternatives are not limited just to perfect wisdom and cloddish ignorance. Suffering lessens and happiness increases when we make an effort to follow the Noble Eightfold Path, whatever our present condition. In the classic formula, the Dhamma is "visible here and now, of immediate result, inviting to come and see, onward-leading, directly experienceable by the wise" (*Aṅguttara Nikāya* III, 53–54). *Nibbāna* is the supreme freedom to which the Dhamma leads, and the closer we approach that goal the freer we will become.

Perhaps we cannot see *Nibbāna* resplendent right before us, but we can certainly make out the ground beneath our feet; we can know when we draw a joyful breath or put behind us an old sorrow or refrain from a spiteful act or compose an agitated mind. The Dhamma gives benefits in the present as well as in the future. Is there not satisfaction in performing a good deed with a clear mind? Is there not uplift in a moment of quiet contemplation saved from the uproar of the day? The Dhamma lightens our burdens in the present and gives us reason for hope.

What then does this have to do with the problems of romantic love? Simply this: The Dhamma puts the delights and torments of love into perspective, so that we can break the illusion of love as the highest of aspirations and most essential of desires. Paradoxically, such disillusionment is the key to treating others better, with true benevolence and a sympathetic understanding of human needs. Ordinarily we believe—and most of mankind seems to take for granted—that love is an innate, spontaneous skill that merely requires suitable objects and opportunities, a skill that we might practice with perfect success irrespective of any blemishes on our character or deficiencies in our understanding. But no virtue can stand in isolation; no fruit can reach full sweetness without adequate water and soil and sunlight. The facets of human life are mutually dependent and mutually conditioned. Thus, to act with consistent goodness we must set about becoming worthy persons, and to do that we must recognize reliable principles and shape our thoughts, words, and deeds accordingly. And how shall we accomplish that without effort? We have instincts for bad as well as for good, so we ought not to count on luck alone. We must know ourselves before we presume to know another and demand quotas of romance, tenderness, and attention.

By knowing ourselves in the practice of the Noble Eightfold Path we can come to contest the supposed supremacy of passion. How could a trembling, mercurial mass of emotions be the richest of treasures? It cannot match the serenity and purity of *Nibbāna*, which does not change and does not disappoint. If love is to refresh us and uplift us at all it must be realistically considered and not fantastically worshipped. Through the day-to-day practice of basic virtues it should be made better, made sound, made right. To do that we should examine all its aspects in ourselves and discard the unhelpful—the admixtures of conceit, greed, self-importance, etc. Our ambiguous motives require sharp attention. Are we mostly intent on giving or receiving? Conscious of the world-transcending Dhamma, of the incomparable release of *Nibbāna*, we should raise our standards and purify our conduct in all respects, both for our own advancement and for the pleasing of others. Gold in its natural state is full of impurities, but the goldsmith refines it, cleanses it, purifies it, works it into a state of beauty and luster. Similarly, the follower of the Dhamma takes his own compassionate and kindly tendencies and purifies them, improves them, and works them into something better.

Understanding and practice of the Dhamma do not destroy our capacity to love or appreciate love—far from it. The Dhamma can purge the grasping, selfish qualities from our love and make it purer and nobler. As we come to understand through personal experience the rightness and goodness of the path of Dhamma, we may also discover, slowly or suddenly, that the voracious desires we previously thought to be the only purposes for our existence are really not so, and that something of wondrous value surpasses them—indistinct as yet but flashing out now and again from the clouds of possibility. When we lean hard, seeking to take and keep, we will fall hard—such is the nature of grasping. But when we do not lean, when instead we hold ourselves upright, looking at the world with an undeflected eye, the good will we have flows out of us without weakening us. This is *mettā*—loving kindness without selfishness. It becomes purer as we realize it is not the purest; it becomes happier as we realize it is not the happiest. *Nibbāna* surpasses all.

If, through our own ripening knowledge, we recognize that our ultimate and highest purpose as conscious beings should be *Nibbāna*, the absolute end of greed, hatred, and delusion, then all goals beneath that take on a new and truer coloring. When we have something to live for that is higher than fame, wealth, comfort, or health—higher even than love—we can never be utterly impoverished or ruined. We are then in fact in a much better position to enjoy whatever may be intelligently achieved in life because we no longer depend solely on changeable circumstances for our happiness. Minds change, passions cool, opportunities disappear, quarrels flare up, calamities separate us from the good and the worthy; so if we are to escape repeated grief we must not go on investing ourselves vainly and obsessively in what is perishable. We need to keep our minds, and consequently our actions, as free as possible from craving and attendant defilements. While we cannot cut off these harmful conditions at once by an act of will, we can certainly loosen their frightful grip on us by following the path and paying attention to the deliverance that shines at its end.

Love is never the poorer for being accompanied by wisdom. It is not harmed by being denied a crown. The agonies we endure and inflict in the name of love come from making love bear too heavy a weight, from recklessly heaping our ambitions, fears, desires, and loneliness on top of another person—another who is as changeable as we. It is natural to form attachments to other people, but the pain produced from these attachments will vary according to our wisdom and maturity. If we see nothing higher at all and plunge thoughtlessly into the conflict of gaining and losing, we will surely suffer, but if we keep the ideals of the Dhamma before us, peacefully contemplating the transience of things, we will ride more securely over the waves of fortune.

According to Buddhism, everything that has the characteristic of arising also has the characteristic of ceasing, so it is best to set our aim on *Nibbāna*, that deliverance beyond all concepts and limits that does not arise and thus does not cease—does not fluctuate with the momentary universe. An independent mind, aspiring to this deliverance, is not a chilly, unfeeling mind, but a mind whose goodness is uncalculated, beneficent, free—less and less shaken by the furious hunger of ego. If we keep the windows of the mind open to the streaming light of Dhamma then that light will bathe our thoughts and actions and distinguish the skillful from the foolish.

Even without understanding of the Dhamma most of us will distinguish in theory between mere superficial attraction and true love. We think of superficial attraction or whimsical desire as capricious, irresponsible, and shallow, and true love as mature, serious, and steady—although in life it is hard to tell where one ends and the other begins. At least we recognize some advantage in clear sight and reflection, and this recognition grows sharper with training in the Dhamma. We must become less inclined to throw ourselves at the feet of an admired person and more prepared to stand up straight, honest, mindful, ready to meet our fortune bravely. To a world that knows nothing loftier than the convulsions of craving this might seem a loss, but one who truly experiences the refreshment of wisdom will gather the strength to throw off fear and selfishness and gain a peace surpassing all earthly calculations.

Romantic love reaches its natural expression in marriage—the formal commitment of two people to share their lives, to trust and take care of one another—but this is by no means an automatic process. Marriage does not ensure the continuation of love but only the opportunity for it. As always in the Buddhist view, blessings depend on conditions, and appear or disappear according to the nature of our thoughts, words, and deeds. Just as we cannot rely on love as an abstract power to make us happy, we cannot count on marriage simply as an institution that will relieve us of the daily necessity to work hard to get along with someone else. The satisfactions and joys of spouse, children, and family are products both of affection and intelligence: a person loves and tries rationally to adjust to another person's needs. The elemental attraction between the sexes cannot by itself maintain a harmonious relationship. Understanding, tolerance, thoughtfulness, tact, and a host of other virtues and talents are required of husband and wife every day, until it becomes plain—or should become plain—that the perfection of love means, ultimately, the perfection of one's own character.

Thus we are brought back once again to the Dhamma, to the examination of our own flaws and the need to overcome them. We cannot repair our defects by ignoring them or blithely assigning them to the care of another; we cannot love wisely as long as we pretend we have no other duties. It is the noble person who can truly benefit others as well as himself, so we ought to be intent on the path leading to nobility.

So uncertain is the world and so changeable the mind that even under advantageous circumstances there is no guarantee that love will be returned satisfactorily, or at all, or that it will last long, or that it will produce nothing but joy. When we depend on it *entirely* for our happiness we must tremble in the shadow of pain, however agreeable our seeming security. What if we should lose our heart's support tomorrow? We are safe as long as we have each other, we assure ourselves dreamily. But how long will that be? Dissension, time, distance, change, or finally death dissolves all alliances, plunging the unwary into despair and desolation; and if we have no wisdom we too may go drifting about the lonely streets with our eyes staring desperately into other eyes and seeing the same desperation there.

When we suffer the pains of broken love it helps to reflect on the impermanence not just of love but of those very pains. They are transitory phenomena, not self, with no more power to harm us than what we surrender to them. Plundering time, which wrenches from us what we cherish, breaks up also our present misery, and the more easily as we resolve to practice patience. With mindfulness well established we can refrain from adding new momentum to upset feelings. When a boat sails across a lake, the churning wake spreads out, subsides, and vanishes with natural ease. What purpose would there be in trying to keep the waters stirred up? The lake left undisturbed grows calm again.

In the way of the Buddha we can find relief from distress and grief; in wisdom there is security. Because love is fragile it cannot protect us forever, but if we relax our grip it may bloom even better, allowing us to give and receive without encumbrance, frenzy, or fear, offering to each other our strength instead of our weakness. When we have *Nibbāna* as our highest goal we gain freedom in our relationships now; we will not suffocate one another; we will be glad to help one another along the path.

In a sense the practice of Dhamma is like gradually filling the abyss of ignorance with knowledge until that terrible vacuum is neutralized and the heart cries no more for unknown comfort. The loving kindness of the perfected one, who has grown wise by experience and reflection, is just the over-measure, the radiance of his goodness, quite purified of vacillation, selfishness, and visceral wanting.

While we cannot instantly do away with our weaknesses, we can consciously elevate our intentions, straighten our conduct, and contemplate the virtues of the Buddha and the noble ones who are free from craving. Their achievement is an image to set before our inner eye, something higher to live for, within and beyond the motions of our conventional business. No good thing prospers long in ignorance. The better we understand this flawed universe the more skillfully we can live, and the happier we will be. We love best when we do not love out of desperation.

5. *Floodtime*

🍃 AFTER THE SNOW AND THE MELTING, after the long cold rains, the river swells and bulges over its banks, changing the shape of the country. Old islands go awash or under; the shore crags are made islands; marshy woodlands become new channels for the river. We scout for landmarks but this mingling of earth and water makes us wonder if we remember rightly, if the flood has not obliterated time or cast the world far back to its muddy beginnings. We stand here where spring has not quite begun, in the pale, primeval sun and north wind, and our senses swing like the needle of a shaken compass. What does the fluttering of our consciousness signify? All this thinking, this habitual noise we take as a self, seems lost in the greater speech of nature around us—or would be lost, perhaps, if we could let go of it now, so immense and strange is the change of the tumbling river.

There used to be a path along this bank, or a boulder of memorable shape, or a tangle of vines, or a grove of beeches with mysterious shade. Where are they? We gaze at the cold spines of alien forest and the maze of waters, and there is little that seems familiar. A woodpecker raps out a theme on dead wood high in the air: "Lost! Lost! Lost!" Or maybe it is only the wild vibration of things in their true state, quite innocent of messages. Today is neither winter nor spring, neither cloudy nor clear—just a place and a moment stripped to the bone, all markers disarrayed, the very words in our minds flapping like rags on a thorn.

Just over a little hill (if we did not dream it) highways and electric wires tie the world together, and there waits the routine we came from and to which we mean to return. But here it is harsh floodtime and the river has risen, dragging the beaches away, shoving flotsam up the banks, bending the willows, overrunning the lowlands, and pouring as well through the hearts of all mindful watchers. If the woods are strange and the shoreline desolate, if stone, earth, and wood may be so scoured and changed, so must be the frail, ticking life of human beings. Around us in this hour the elements are not storming, but we come to feel a wrench half of fear, half of exhilaration, as if the river promises to smash the nest of our opinions and scatter all the little twigs away.

Clumsy and short of breath in our erratic rambling, we wonder at the manifest impermanence of nature—the caved banks of streams, the wrecked log bridge, the deep silt over last year's picnics. In floodtime we see everywhere the upset of the ordinary and remember that the human creature with its seemingly important business has the same destiny as the floating clots of leaves. The sliding sky and dissolving earth put to shame the impertinence of imagining, *I am this, I have that, I will do as I like.* What shall we ever stir but a few puffs of dust? What do we know, really, but the trivial murmur of our own puny thoughts?

Still, in the clean air of the vast, restless season, in the awesome and refreshing solitude, a rare free mood springs up quivering like a candle flame. Together with the metamorphosing country we are changing whether we like it or not, and in this instant our history seems trivial and the day's prospects infinite. We stand shifting our feet on the soft ground and wondering if something is required of us besides patience, wondering if we could escape the swamp of appearances and someday find our peace in a new, unsorrowing country.

Maybe we would just wait and dream of deliverance as we always have done, but today the sun is unstable and the wind sharp. Must we not come to terms with floodtime as it is? Are we still marooned in fantasies, disoriented by the mind's unceasing internal flood? We seem to be engaged in laboriously translating the ineffable facts of experience into crude symbols of thought and speech—a tiring business—and if only the sun would burn a little warmer we might bound up the staircase of our desire into the heavens. But the barbarous icy waters have despoiled the banks, drowned the fields, invaded the woods—so from where shall we start climbing? Beauty and ugliness, hope and despair, liking and disliking are swirling before us in the muddy current of the river, waiting to be pulled out and molded into an ordinary life once again. But we are weary of them; they have never given us the shelter we longed for. Where then shall we turn? Like other small, routed creatures of the shore, we are caught in a crisis, ready to migrate but fearful of the change.

Self-esteem, back in the remembered world, depended on being noticed, on keeping up the fiction that we are important, substantial, and admirable, but out here the wind and the sun and the great wet earth esteem nothing and notice nobody. It is just a fresh, free day at the beginning of ages, and whoever goes wandering through these woods had best leave all baggage behind. Our notion of self has become a grievous burden that sinks our heels in mud and oppresses our hearts with a thousand imperatives. We must nurse, protect, and entertain this self, acquiesce to its appetites and aversions, and constantly affirm its worth and preeminence. But what good will it do us when we try to leap these streams of floodtime? Watching the country swept away before us, we sense the triviality and falseness of the self and wonder if it would be possible to expunge it entirely from our thoughts, to shrug off the weight of delusion, and at once rise to a level above all floods. Perhaps the heart goes a little faster, the imagination swims with possibilities. Even an undesired crisis might be turned to a blessing.

Where shall we go? Where to direct the mind? We have our theories but maybe they are only so much conceit, only cobwebs thrown to catch a leviathan. Does the world offer us any clues? If we watch and listen intently we may be sure that it does. The woodpecker with its on-and-off knocking, the mix of sun and shadow in the woods, the dry beech leaves buzzing in the wind, the busy water carving earth— they all declare the nature of things; they all preach true Dhamma.

Cut off for now from manufactured comforts, wrenched by the turn of seasons, we cannot suppress the upwelling of a question; we cannot keep from blurting to the unconscious river, *Why am I so lost?* And with the words loosed and blown across the sky like leaves, we find ourselves already drawn on to track down an answer, as if the admission of our ignorance somehow commits us to the search for wisdom. Reflecting on all this chaotic change in nature, we see that the instability runs deeper than we imagined, that we who are wondering about the fleeting show are ourselves rushed on like sticks in the flood. It becomes impossible—as we scan the distances, as we inspect the spinning flotsam, as we review our thoughts—to find anything that does not change and pass away. We have till now given so little attention to this universal flux that we have failed to understand the laws that work upon us and, being slothful or indifferent or simply careless, we have again and again crashed against huge, frightening questions of pain and longing. Now, in this wilderness of time, a flood has orphaned us on a strange beach that is itself crumbling into the stream, and wet nature repeats to our senses what we might have learned long before as doctrine: "All formations are impermanent." It was one thing to read the words in the quiet of our rooms and another to stand here cold and beleaguered in the midst of unstoppable change.

We can go back, of course, back to the semi-oblivion of amusements, but that will not resolve the crisis, only hide it for a time. Or we can attend to the Dhamma and begin to make our way across the wilderness toward security. All formations are impermanent—a somber thought! And yet an invigorating one. All landscapes and edifices, pleasure and laughter, dreams and fancies—all, by minutes and centuries, are collapsing, wilting, re-forming, becoming different. All formations are suffering. So said the Buddha, and so we come to see as we study the mortal flaws in all we value and in all we regard as mere background. Then if formations of mind and matter are impermanent, and if they are flawed and unsatisfactory, what should we think of the airiest confection of all—this self or ego? How it weighs upon us when we cannot even see it or touch it or demonstrate its reality! All things, said the Buddha, are nonself. The mighty "I" we have served so long is a mere figure of speech, a massive nothing, and when we cling to it we stagger beneath an imagined burden; we groan under delusion.

We do not like to think of ourselves as deluded (though we suspect our neighbors of that failing) but in the abstract, at least, it is not hard to understand that if we have to some extent misapprehended or misinterpreted our experience, then the theories we have constructed and relied upon may actually be misleading us. We are accustomed to blaming other people or external forces for our confusion because it is more agreeable to do so than to examine the disconcerting possibility that our own minds are faulty. We realize we do not have perfect bodies that are impervious to illness or frailty, yet we assume we have minds that consistently and adeptly grasp reality. We believe we have a self or are a self of some kind, and since it is *I* we are reluctant to consider that it might be changeable, confused, amorphous, and ultimately illusory. Thus we become confirmed in error.

Seeking for a self among the processes of mind and body is like seeking for an entity called "music" among or within the musicians and instruments of an orchestra. When they have stopped playing we might step forward and demand to see the source or hiding place of the symphony we have just heard. We have experienced music, so we might insist that it exists on its own as a discrete *thing*; and yet, when we come to look, all we can find is an assortment of people, chairs, instruments, and pieces of paper. We cannot find any germ or nugget of "symphony" curled inside a horn or a violin, or nesting in a musician's pocket, or squeezed between the pages of the score. Obviously, there is no self to a piece of music; it comes into being depending on many conditions—the work of a composer, written directions, machines for production of sound, the efforts of the players, etc.—and ceases when those conditions are dispersed. In the same way, the self or ego we think we are exists only in a manner of speaking, only in a conventional and illusory sense; ultimately no "I" can be found—only a compound of factors working together temporarily.

A person, a living being, can be described as *nāma-rūpa*—mentality and material form. Mentality is a collection of processes of perceiving, knowing, thinking, desiring, willing, etc. Material form here is the physical, material aspect of a person—the gross substance of the body with its physical properties. These two mutually supportive aspects act together to carry out the functions of life. *Nāma* (mentality) forms an intention and *rūpa* (material form) walks; *nāma* is hungry and *rūpa* eats.

47

The eye receives light and the mind experiences vision. Mentality by itself lacks motive power. Material form, or body, can sit, stand, walk, eat when directed, but it cannot know or feel or understand anything. Both the mental and the material are impersonal and selfless. Through their combination there comes to be the complex of activities we call sentient life.

This is one way of looking at the make-up of the person who now hikes along the soggy bank and wonders at the make-up of the river. The Buddha's analysis goes further, describing life in terms of five aggregates or groups (*khandhas*): material form or body (*rūpa* again) along with four mental aggregates—feeling, perception, mental formations, and consciousness. These are not enduring, independent entities of any kind—just classes of processes constantly changing. The Buddha analyzes them, moreover, into various subclasses, explaining their particular functions, pointing out their interdependent nature and their emptiness or impersonality. The person is a built-up, ever-changing compound of activities in which no security, permanence, or self can be found; therefore one who wishes release from sorrow—escape from the flood—must give up the profitless clinging to shadows and learn to look with objectivity. The Buddha shows that whatever is impermanent is fundamentally unreliable and unsatisfactory, and that whatever is impermanent and unsatisfactory cannot reasonably be taken as a self, an enduring identity. Accordingly a new attitude toward all these aggregates is called for:

> *Therefore, monks, any material form whatsoever...any feeling...any perception...any formations...any consciousness whatsoever, whether past, future or present, in oneself or external, coarse or fine, inferior or superior, far or near, should all be regarded as it actually is by right understanding thus: "This is not mine, this is not what I am, this is not my self."*

(Vinaya Mahāvagga 1:6)

Our life is far more complex, compounded, and dynamic than we have been accustomed to think. As long as we defend the supposed durability and reality of the "I" we afflict our minds with delusion and continue to misunderstand the world and to suffer. Events stream past in chaos and pain because we try to set this "I" apart and preserve it from the universal cycle of arising and passing away. But there is nothing here to be preserved but delusion. We build a fortress of selfhood out of passionate ignorance but are forced to watch its walls wrecked again and again by woes and griefs—and with ancient desperation, knowing no better, we rebuild with the same wretched bricks.

If we can seriously take up the provocative idea that our "self" is only a sort of fiction, can we discover a new way to live? If we are mistaken in claiming a solitary, durable identity should we instead try, somehow, to merge with the rest of the universe, to attach our personality to a greater whole? When a crisis teaches us the folly of trying to deny the transience of phenomena, we turn hopefully to such thoughts, but no satisfaction awaits us here, either. Wherever we house it, an illusion is just that. Since no self is to be found in the first place, we gain nothing by assigning it here or there or reconceiving it as some kind of collective identity. We cannot perceive or lay hold of a self of any dimensions and hence cannot presume to do anything with it. Where there has been no separation there can be no union. That is why, however we yearn and strain here in the weak, mystical sunlight, we will not go floating away on heavenly breezes. We have to keep working on this problematical earth.

With the crisis, the floodtime, suddenly upon us, with nature tremendously illustrating the Dhamma, we might feel simultaneously our loneliness and our connection with other living beings. Our emancipation is our own responsibility, not to be won for us by others, not even by the Buddha; but we can and should help others, whose plight and whose inmost hopes we share and from whom we are not, after all, separated by shells of selfhood. Our confusion, we should understand from the Buddha's teaching, does not spring from a crazy, random universe but from our own disordered minds. If we will strive to keep down the destructive self-illusion we will enable our minds to see more directly and accurately.

What then does the balanced mind see? It sees things in their actual nature; that is, as impermanent, unsatisfactory, and entirely empty of self or ego. It sees, without bias or passion, the coming and going of conditioned phenomena. What then becomes of the person, of "me"? Is the person one thinks oneself to be in fact nonexistent? Few of us relish the idea of nonexistence. But the problem is only apparent, a result of the way we misinterpret our experiences. A human being exists as a dynamic combination of material form, feeling, perception, mental formations, and consciousness. There is no need—and no room—for a despotic ego or self. When the conceit of self has been eradicated by deep insight, impurities such as greed, hatred, and delusion no longer have a point to stick to, no longer a foothold for destructiveness. When the heart becomes light and pure and certain it will not sink in any flood.

The teachings of Buddhism are carried by words, by symbols that point to living verities in forest and river, mind and matter. To see these verities is to see the Dhamma, and to see the Dhamma is to see the Buddha. Both timelessly point toward deliverance—past all the ditches and fences of opinion toward a pure landscape uncontaminated by self-conceit. Words and experience are not the same, but they are complementary, together impelling us on the path to liberation. What we need is neither intellectual mastery nor mindless abstraction, but a vivid understanding born from the application of our faculties to the roiling world before us. All blooming, fading, changing, flying phenomena preach true Dhamma, but they preach only to the listening, ready mind. Our duty must be to listen and understand and act in faith.

Because we are alive and conscious, because we dwell in continual contradiction between desires and results, we must from time to time face a crisis—the convergence of great currents within us, the breakdown of pretense, the momentary clearing of our eyes. Then we have to make our choices, whether to retire deeper into diversions until the shudder of uncertainty passes, or to set out on the wild waters of knowledge on the raft of Dhamma. Within us the ghost of self urges retreat, and yet, having glimpsed a little of those far, clean spaces, how could we give up now? What faith is it that never builds to action? What courage that never engages fear?

Along the riverbank the world seems scarcely begun. Green buds are fat but unburst, the climbing vines asleep in the tree limbs they will soon decorate, the birds few and sweet-voiced. But the great river is at work undermining the roots of trees. Some have fallen to the surging flood; more will fall. The rushing, sighing, pouring sounds fill up space almost like silence, fill up the observer and the observed. Where are we now? It is floodtime, a raw, new day, and we have this moment to reflect, this transparent moment when we stand and listen and make no noise and concoct no frantic dreams. But nature will not pause and the river will not cease from flowing, and we must act. Now in a chattering of twigs and leaves the wind comes at us through the forest, fierce and cold and turbulent with life.

6. Other Travelers

🍃 THE PRACTICE OF BUDDHISM should lead us out of self-absorption in more ways than one. The "untaught ordinary person" (as the Pali texts frankly put it) has a misguided love for himself or herself and as a consequence a misguided and very imperfect love for other creatures. The world, in our preferred arrangement, is peopled chiefly with "me" and secondarily with others who provide conflict, interest, diversion, and finally definition of a substantial universe. Narrowly imagining our own benefit, we tend to regard other beings benevolently to the extent that they accommodate us and please us; we hate them to the extent that they block our will. What could be more natural? This is our habit, our tradition, which insight must penetrate and annul.

It should become apparent even to the novice on the Buddhist path that ordinary notions of self and what should belong to self are impediments to understanding and eventual liberation. Buddhist moral discipline, philosophy, and meditation all aim at undercutting and destroying these notions. Living beings are streams of transitory physical and mental events that, though different in outward characteristics, have the same nature of ignorance and confusion rushing through birth and death with no unchanging center apparent anywhere. Distinctions between living creatures being impermanent and mutable, it follows that practitioners of the Dhamma should try to avoid false self-regard and act with good will toward others for everyone's benefit; indeed in Buddhist literature we find many exhortations to compassion and friendliness. Writers of all ages have rightly praised the virtue of love for one's fellow man but have had less to say about those other beings near us, who share the same physical environment. Those others are of course animals.

As long as we assume that only human life has any significance, and as long as we determinedly look at the world in terms of "I" and what supports or opposes "me" we are still engaged in misperception; and our sense of charity is likely to prove inconsistent and casual and unproductive of any deeper reflection or thorough moral improvement. It is not so hard for a sensitive and well-intentioned person to feel some degree of sympathy for other living creatures, especially affectionate pets or other beautiful or interesting animals; but to see those other creatures as morally significant beings in their own right and to treat them with considered benevolence is somewhat more difficult and requires attention.

In the case of animals we have a good opportunity to contemplate moral complexities, because animals are patently different from us and yet they share this earth with us and give evidence of being sentient beings with desires and emotions similar to our own. In Buddhism charity toward animals is not a by-product of human ethics but a part of our general moral duty to all living, suffering beings, as all are caught in the wheel of birth and aging and death (*saṃsāra*)—all of us going on from life to life in various forms, in various planes of existence ranging from woeful, wretched states to exalted, heavenly planes. There is no permanence, no staying forever in any one of these planes, and no assured progression from lower to higher. The Buddha teaches that existence is an endless wandering conditioned by the deeds one performs: good deeds tend to produce fortunate rebirth and bad deeds tend to produce unfortunate rebirth—on and on until or unless one attains enlightenment—the release to *Nibbāna*.

From the potency of enough accumulated bad deeds we could be born as animals, and perhaps have been innumerable times through uncountable aeons. Human life—speaking generally—is a fortunate situation, whereas animal life is an unfortunate one, bereft of intelligence and stricken with heavy suffering. Still, all unenlightened beings remain fundamentally insecure, subject to pain and death and separation from comforts. We should not, therefore, be complacent about our current satisfactions or neglectful of those generous actions that will help both ourselves and others.

A brief look at some fundamental doctrines should show the depth of Buddhist concern for fellow beings. First of all there is the doctrine of harmlessness (*ahiṃsā*), which permeates the five fundamental moral precepts of the lay Buddhist. We are advised to refrain from (1) killing, (2) taking what is not given, or stealing, (3) sexual misconduct, (4) false speech, and (5) taking intoxicants. Bearing in mind the first precept, the devout Buddhist is harmless; he or she does no intentional harm to living beings. Killing enemies is not all right. Hunting animals for food or sport is not all right. Destroying troublesome creatures might seem expedient, but the doing of harm sets up a liability to future harm for the doer. All creatures desire to live and to escape pain; we are like them; they are like us; they should receive kindness at our hands. Seeing all life as caused and conditioned, changing from this form to that form, one with a peaceable heart will refrain from doing ill to any creature. Human beings are not supreme in the universe; they are, like all other beings, subject to the effects of their own deeds; and misfortune will follow those who indulge in violence and cruelty.

A second doctrine showing Buddhist concern for animals is the fifth factor of the Noble Eightfold Path: right livelihood. In order to live a wholesome life here and now, as well as to attain ultimate liberation, one must have a blameless form of livelihood. Specifically, one should avoid occupations that involve killing, such as hunting, fishing, and slaughtering animals. One should also refrain from trading in arms, living beings, flesh, intoxicants, and poisons. In general terms, no occupation directly connected with doing harm to living beings should be pursued by one anxious to escape suffering and reach enlightenment.

Why is this? Should we cease harming animals, even troublesome animals, simply because the Buddha laid down certain standards? Like all principles of good behavior in Buddhism, those of harmlessness and right livelihood arise from practical considerations. We should avoid certain actions because they naturally lead to suffering for ourselves as well as others. We must give thought to the encompassing law of *kamma* (*karma* in Sanskrit)—the law of moral cause and effect. Good deeds give rise to good results and bad to bad. Or we might say that our intentional actions tend to return to us, sooner or later, for benefit or for harm, depending on the character of those actions. Willfully killing or injuring an animal, even a small or despised animal, even with the approval of others, is an unwholesome act that plants the seeds for future suffering. The degree to which such seeds might ripen for the doer is something impossible to predict—and certainly the moral weight of deeds varies enormously—but we know that if we do no harm we will start no fires of *kamma*, and that if we consistently act with compassion we can look forward to blessings.

Probably only a very small proportion of humanity is consciously, wantonly cruel to animals. After all, human beings cherish their pets. But what about such recreations as hunting and fishing? Must these be given up? Buddhist moral discipline, it should be remembered, is not a set of commands but of precepts—trustworthy guidelines for skillful and graceful living. The Buddha points out the advantages of following them and the painful consequences of ignoring them. Hunting and fishing cause suffering and are not necessary for our livelihood or happiness. It is up to us to choose.

In any discussion of killing there inevitably arises the question of vegetarianism, because in our world animals are killed in great numbers for food. While condemning the killing of living creatures, the Buddha did not categorically prohibit his monks from eating meat, except of a few special kinds, because the bare act of eating is in itself morally neutral. What one eats affects one's physical organs, not one's spiritual standing. Monks, moreover, subsist on the alms given by the laity. Having entered into a dependent, ascetic livelihood, they must make do with whatever food the laity is pleased to offer, using it not out of greed but just to maintain health. The Buddha allowed monks to accept meat when it is offered unless they see, hear, or suspect that an animal has been killed specifically for them. Thus he set practical limits to monastic responsibility. For the laity he made no prohibitions about food. He was a religious teacher concerned with essential religious principles. Full of pity for all beings, the Buddha was concerned to teach his followers those moral truths that would lead them to consistent harmlessness and kindliness of behavior and that would thereby benefit both them and the world at large.

Intentional acts of injuring and killing are reprehensible, and the Buddha was entirely opposed to harming any creature. Those who intentionally kill act wrongly and accumulate demerit for themselves. Studying this position along with the principles of right livelihood, it is clear that in an ideal world there would be no killing and hence no meat eating. But we do not live in such a world and must make our way as best we can in this one. Certainly vegetarianism appeals strongly to many Buddhists nowadays for reasons of health or economics or sentiment; and to the extent that it contributes to peace of mind and body and the welfare of creatures it should be considered beneficial. We must simply remember that voluntary restrictions on diet are external, arbitrary matters, not moral absolutes, which should by no means obscure the need for restraint in our own directly intended actions. Do we kill or not kill? Do we abuse or comfort? Do we wish well or ill? These are the significant moral questions.

Animals suffer abuse in many ways at the hands of human beings, and all of them are deplorable from a Buddhist standpoint. One sort that thrives in our own time is the terrible treatment of animals in scientific laboratories, where multitudes of hapless creatures are made to suffer poisoning, mutilation, and death, purportedly for the eventual benefit of mankind. Anyone with a sense of the interdependence of earthly life and a sympathy for the sufferings of living beings must recoil from the cruelties performed in the name of science. Even if it could be demonstrated that the tormenting of some hundreds or thousands of animals would improve the quality of chemicals or the treatment of some human disease, we would still not be justified in inflicting such pain. In Buddhist teaching the goal in mind does not excuse the method used in reaching for it. Cruelty is never neutralized by reference to some possible future benefit; it rankles unchecked and may erupt in time. *Kamma*, or volitional, intentional action—whether or not one thinks it wrong, whether or not one forgets it—tends to produce appropriate fruit for the doer. Thus anyone concerned for his own welfare should conscientiously refrain from inflicting suffering on living beings.

There remains another large question: what to do about agricultural and domestic pests? It is true that in agriculture it is almost impossible to avoid the death of small creatures, for while one might raise crops without making any attempt to destroy pests (an admirable and difficult task), small creatures may die even in the tilling of soil. Here we must distinguish between intended and unintended action. Intentional killing is always unwholesome to one degree or another, while unintentional or accidental killing is not and does not set up bad consequences in the future. A compassionate and sensible policy, then, is not to do any willful action aimed at killing or harming living creatures. If we remain doubtful about the exact nature of our intentions or are particularly determined not to bring about any harm whatever, even inadvertently, it might be prudent to pursue a different occupation. However, with regard to agriculture or any form of livelihood, we should understand that to prevent all unintended harm that might somehow follow from our actions is surely impossible, and we need not worry about what is beyond our will and our control. We are simply called upon to be vigilant, sympathetic, and restrained—for our own moral advancement and peace and for the well-being of other living creatures.

Apart from matters of livelihood, we sometimes suffer the presence of rodents or insects in our houses and might think it necessary to exterminate them. A thoughtful Buddhist should make an effort to deal with the problem by nonlethal means, such as capturing alive and releasing outside the invading creatures, or using harmless repellents, or preventing access to food and hiding places, or otherwise discouraging the entry of pests into the house. All this requires some trouble and work, of course, but that is the nature of moral discipline. The Buddha knew that we do not immediately have the strength to be saints, but he surely wished us to try as hard as we can to live up to honorable ideals. If we are inclined to make compromises we should pause to consider the Buddha's teachings on harmlessness and *kamma*.

Close observation of animals not only reinforces appreciation of the fragility of life but draws us into a deeper contemplation of our own predicament in the immense revolving cosmos. Here before us legions of living creatures struggle and suffer and die—unfortunate creatures guided only by their immediate impulses, appetites, and pains. Except for a privileged few they will expire miserably, uncared for. They have little understanding and no inheritance but the hard necessity of past action that has brought them to this birth and the instinctive deeds that will send them on to future births that may be just as unfortunate. When they might rise to better states is an uncertain matter depending on the fading out of bad *kamma* and the potency of good.

Even if we—unwisely—discount the danger of being reborn as animals ourselves as a result of unwholesome, demeritorious deeds, we ought to notice that the animal kingdom presents a magnified, intensified picture of our own present condition. For, like animals, we cannot long escape illness and pain; we must sometimes endure deprivation and harsh treatment; we do not comprehend the giant forces that seize us, frighten us sick, and fling us to and fro. There we go, morning after morning, faltering out into the dread world of frustration and jealousy, fed and groomed but no better prepared than ever, pacing our circular path like zoo lions, pathetically awaiting some improvement from *without*—some morsel tossed through the bars. Maybe our captivity is less apparent, our leash less taut, but still we live mastered by habit, not expecting to get out of it, making little feints here and there to sniff the wind, but losing concentration, losing the scent of liberation, deciding instead to scratch and sleep, and waking again in anxiety. Perhaps we strike with sarcasm instead of fangs; yet we can purr in our way; yet we would have in our troubled night some gentle word. We are baffled and long for peace.

Animals at their work or play might amuse us or bore us or disgust us or leave us indifferent. They should instruct us, as indeed should all the phenomena of nature. That squirrel burying nuts in the yard—will it find them again under the snow? We, packing away notes and bonds—will we find them, or find them sustaining, when we grope for meaning and consolation in the rain of misfortune? How much of our industriousness is thoughtless instinct after all? In an era when the sublime Dhamma is still known, and we are born with faculties sufficient to understand it, should we not try to escape the brutish bondage of ignorance?

In the crush of regular responsibilities it would be worthwhile to devote some time to shaping a noble silence, a contemplation of freedom. The world talks at us endlessly, but could we not refrain from adding to the din? Throngs of birds make a twittering uproar in the bushes outside our windows—maybe they are briefly content in their own state, but would we wish it on ourselves? Like flies senselessly butting a windowpane, we are hard to convince to reverse our course, to fly another way to find an opening to freedom. Or like befuddled cows we make pass after pass around the corral in bovine perseverance. If we look about us at the scurrying, sighing, huddling, crying clans of beings, we might see in these flocks and herds and hapless multitudes some of our own sad tendencies come to worse condition.

No power, human or divine, can compel anyone to feel pity. Only a mind roused by wisdom can finally subdue the ancient pounding of self-will and self-assertion. After deliberating on the nature of cause and effect, moral precepts, and injunctions against taking life, after *acting* according to them in good will and faith in the Dhamma, the resolute Buddhist will find the buds of latent compassion opening. One careful for his own welfare must also be careful for the welfare of others, making no petty distinctions of high or low, but appreciating the infinite reach of the Buddha's compassion, the radiance of understanding that overflows the vessel of the single mind and embraces all creatures.

Human beings live in a condition of mixed pleasures and pains where the contradictions of existence stand out starkly, and have, potentially at least, enough mental ability to understand and transcend suffering. A perfected person, having come into knowledge of the relationships between living beings wandering through time, puts no limits on goodness, but directs boundless benevolence toward all who suffer—butterflies, birds, human beings, all. If we would elevate ourselves to such a station—to a liberation beyond all stations—we should take a care now not to injure our fellow wanderers, but to let them live in peace, and for all, in all directions, to wish: May they be safe, may they escape suffering, may they find their way to *Nibbāna*.

7. Earth Tones

For us who are much attached to beautiful colors and shapes, winter makes a problem. We have doted on rich green maples, crimson azalea bushes, and cheery blue skies, and when the turning year drives these dainties away we are at a loss, wondering how to live expansively in a constricted, frozen world. Shall we concentrate on an indoor hobby, or fly to the tropics? The live colors that sustained us have died back to browns, to the whites of snow-dust, to the infinite range of grays, and we look out the windows of our speeding cars—our bubbles of warmth—onto a blasted land. These dormant, muddy farms, these austere forests, these grim cities, these sullied skies—they repel us; they give us nothing; they furnish no entertainment for the senses. We dearly love beauty, but beauty is forever dying, from the rose in the vase by the window to the fragrant acre of wildflowers. In time all forms and colors shrink back to their roots, leaving the senses nothing to feast on, and we squint out of our parkas at the bleak and the dreary with a teeth-chattering stoicism. It is the famine of delight.

But color has subtleties we might forget amid the dramatic hues of spring, summer, and fall. In the great retrenchment of November the available colors grow dimmer and demand a finer eye, until for long months the visible world at these latitudes is mostly resolved to earth tones. From the color of bricks to the color of slate, from bleached grass to brown, drab woods, from tawny dirt to gray, blown rain—the spectrum turns dull. It takes an effort to appreciate the beauty in these humble shades and to find satisfaction in impoverished elements. Indeed, to mine aesthetic pleasure where none apparently is to be found is an achievement of sorts. To note the spare loveliness of a dry weed suggests a fine sensibility. To admire the pattern of a pine tree against a snow bank bespeaks a readiness to rejoice. But on many occasions—when the bullying wind bangs into our faces and when sleet spatters miserably on our heads—we are less eager to poeticize.

It is a season of travel, without and within. Our cars race along a gray track between brown immensities. Where has all the vivid color gone—into the air, evaporated like ether? Scenes run by in miles of drab futility on the old, bare, unwelcoming earth. We see ourselves rushing between points—home and work, engagements and appointments, hope and grief—and somehow the lack of color in the season now reminds us of the somberness of it all. We travel by car between cities or on foot just down to the mailbox and huff our little breaths into the void, while around us the despoiled land spreads away in stone color and dirt color, and the winds hiss and shrill.

Then we go traveling within, and the journey is the same, as if all parts of nature have strangely come to share the same weary tone or value. When the objective world seems empty of delight, we turn, demoralized, to the mind itself and find a corresponding hollowness. Swinging about and around, we might then begin to realize the extent of our dependence on factors beyond our control. Withhold the rain and we wither; strip the maples and we grieve. We plod on toward the future, embittered by loss and uncertain of gain, while the dimmed colors of the landscapes within and without suggest our nearness to the stark elements of snow, dust, wood, and stone. We are used to little jubilations, to the smack of green on our eyes, and without them we feel our mortality close and cold.

But let us look a little deeper. What is the real nature of our appetite for beauty? Is it simply a coarse hunger for the tawdry and the garish? Surely not. If asked, we would probably mumble something about harmony and balance and proportion. We do not really require that nature always flaunt splendid colors. Where then should we draw a line between the cheerful and the gloomy? Color is never entirely gone, but in the poorest times turns ascetic, returns to the earth. The gross appetite will be thwarted but a finer vision picks out agreeable tones in ice, eroded earth, rain-darkened boards, gravel in streams, and drifts of old leaves. We can, if need be, cut our rations of beauty down to ascetic levels. We can by skill and diligence pick up the scraps of old color, harvesting a restorative beauty in unlikely places. This sensibility lives in the human mind and may be strengthened by exercise.

But admiration of beauty by itself will not support us long. However great our fortitude, winter in nature and in fortune will shake us and unsettle us. It will kill the sapling in the yard and let the Arctic into our hearts, making us brood on our defeats and failures. How long can we live on meager dreams, hunched over against the wind and against the reverses of everyday life? Sooner or later our resolve weakens and we find ourselves grieving for lost love, lost beauty, and victory never attained. However dear the object, the longing for it is pain.

The cold seasons of the earth or the mind may be ameliorated by appreciating what beauty there is left, but repeated experience should teach us that we live still with old, ignorant habits that upset tranquility. Might it be possible to break them? Because colors and enjoyments fade we must learn to watch judiciously and cut back our grasping. The world of the senses, for all its charms, is an impermanent world, disappointing and bereaving us when we clutch at it in the belief that it will shelter us forever. As it changes we must get by with lesser or different shelter; we must make do with earth tones; we must live on little. And when that little is gone, what then? If we examine ourselves carefully, we may come to see that the attachment to beautiful, pleasurable things is an impediment to happiness, and that in fact all possessiveness is a blight. Pleasant colors, sounds, smells, tastes, touches, and mental concoctions have no endurance; for all their excitement and allure they vanish and betray us. So how could we look to them for our preservation? Should we not instead try to free ourselves from dependence on changeable objects?

Beauty changes. What arises slides out of sight. In the moment of seizing an object we set ourselves up for suffering because we will sooner or later be separated from that object. Thirsting, reaching, gaining, and losing make a cycle of pain whose intensity varies with the underlying greed. Therefore those who can restrain their senses, who can gracefully adapt to earth tones, will fare much better than those who again and again hunger for delicious sensation. Where there is craving or aversion there will always be suffering, for the mind that pulls or pushes cannot come to balance. Here in this unreliable universe we can neither make the beloved stay nor the undesired disappear, so we will be thwarted wherever we turn as long as we turn with the cycle of liking and disliking.

To transcend the immense spectrum of unsatisfactoriness demands a major redirection of our sensibilities. We need to develop detachment, to cultivate independence of mind as the only defense against universal transience. Mere stoicism fails, because it does not touch the ignorance that lies beneath all craving and thus cannot subdue the pain of decay and loss. To hold ourselves grimly aloof by force alone is little improvement over dashing forward or shrinking back; it still suggests bias, an ignorant desire to preserve ourselves in this or that inevitably temporary condition. Detachment is altogether a different quality—a healthy, knowing neutrality that prevents the arising of fever and anguish.

Such detachment can be gradually won through the systematic practice of mindfulness, that impartial observation that divests objects of superficial fascinations and shows them in their elemental nature. To be detached means to view things calmly and knowingly without becoming entangled in them. We need not prefer dead roses to blooming ones, but we must surely take note of the living and the dead without immediately and compulsively relating them to our self-interest. Seeing things simply as they are gradually neutralizes habitual passions, because we come to learn through experience that *all* conditioned things are caught up in the process of arising and ceasing, and thus the conventional descriptions we apply to objects—as beautiful, ugly, desirable, repulsive, and so on—are ephemeral and unreliable. If we understand this, how shall we presume to extract durable happiness from mere colors or sounds or tastes or other fleeting aspects of changing sensation?

Observing the world and its changes mindfully, with detachment, leads to disenchantment and peace and eventually liberation from suffering—*Nibbāna*. In order to restrain the reflex of greed it is important to try to stop looking at things crudely as potential enjoyments, and to see them more as means for understanding. As long as we unthinkingly surrender to objects the power to infatuate or distract us or to force us into rash action, we live in peril, because of their inherent instability; but if we view with detachment both the repulsive and the lovely, if we see things exactly as they are and not as we would like them to be, then we can live safely and independently. Then the ravenous hunger for experience will not be temporarily sated but dissolved entirely. The eye receives forms, the ear receives sounds, but the idea of grasping them need not arise. The leaves of the forest will fall in their own time and the lakes will freeze over and the birds will come and go—and so should the wise observer be equally in accord with nature.

Have we left beauty behind? Are we dealing now with abstractions, with bloodless ideals? Life without craving does not mean a parched intellectualism or immobility. To be free of the tyranny of the senses—including the mind-sense—is to walk with mindfulness in the present moment, to think, act, and feel without distortion, to be unruffled and capable. Moreover, we do not destroy or despise beauty. Only the feverish *attachment* to beauty is a hazard; that is what we must forsake. When autumn burns itself up and gives way to ashen winter, we will not be dismayed if we have not bound ourselves to the charming show. When a pleasure is spent we may let it pass without grief. Forms, fragrances, colors, and sounds come and go, come and go— that is their nature—while the serenity built within stays undisturbed. Beauty is a poison only if we swallow it; when we use it as the ground for reflection it may prove gracious and inspiring.

If we can turn from reds and greens to earth tones and find beauty there, if we can further train ourselves to appreciate the shades and patterns in tree bark or the subtly overlapping clouds, what might this tell us about the nature of beauty? Do we simply compose it in our minds? Why this unseemly lust for the indefinable? Mindfulness leads us away from thoughtless hunger for stimulation to keener and keener knowledge, to a fine disinterest in the attractions of objects, until they no longer catch at us like brambles or hang on us like burs.

Now over there, glimpsed by chance, a few stalks of pale yellow grass quake in the wind above the snow-crust. In the poverty of winter we bend toward them and meet a surprising beauty in their simple form. Then we are perhaps moved to see them as emblems of impermanence and loss, death and renewal. Then in the deepening silence as the words die away we may pass over the symbol to the pure, unadorned fact: sparse grasses in the frozen field. Here cogitation ends, and only contemplation can carry on. Grass is only grass—let it tremble and blow as it will—and stone is stone and earth is earth, unhated and undesired beneath the great gray wonder of the winter sky.

At these latitudes the season of snow is long, but the season of spiritual cold is longer still for us if we have not learned to let alone what we cannot control and kindle instead a warmth in the heart. Even after April has opened its colors we might feel a residual chill, knowing that the beauties we admire cannot last, that we ourselves cannot. So we live uneasily in the expectation of loss that the next winter will confirm. With detachment, on the other hand, with insight and equanimity, we might walk out on the temperate plains of nondelusion and watch the passage of things with serenity. Nothing really belongs to us in this tempest of sensation, in this figure of trembling matter. Owning nothing, laying claim to nothing, how could we be bereft?

Our cars whine over the roads; our shoes skip over the hard ground; our minds yearn after dreams; but still the sky crawls and the horizon keeps its distance. We travel swiftest when we cease to hurry, when we muse on the leafless maples while they shine with ice and let the summer come back when it will. When we face barrenness and wreckage, when the momentary world presents itself in earth tones, in colors of things antique and elemental, we must bravely make of such stuff a life. This is the now, endlessly renewed, arising and departing. Already, it seems, a scent of gathering spring puffs in from southern latitudes, and clouds, turf, and sea freshen and move on. So the year goes by, and so a fair stillness comes, even as the wind blows and the slow rain drips from the eaves of our house.

8. Age and Wisdom

🌿 THE LENGTH OF OUR PARTICULAR human life is unknown to us but limited, subject to the law of impermanence that governs all phenomena. Certainly none of us will forever possess health and strength to do as we wish, and yet, to many young people and perhaps even to some of the middle-aged, the possibility of actually getting old seems so distant as to be practically inconceivable. People, to the innocent eye of youth, occupy fixed compartments of age and situation. There are small children, the sick, the elderly—and then, quite distinct from all of them, there is "I"—timelessly youthful, energetic, sparkling with ideas and enthusiasms. What could be more natural? Childhood remains in memory, of course, but only as jerky scenes of a movie that has sped on to this climax of young adulthood, where one can amuse oneself indefinitely and achieve wonderful things. If Granddad or Grandma is moving slow, that is no surprise: they've always been old, haven't they? Some people are and some aren't, after all. The polite youth will be glad to give them his arm when they slowly climb the front steps, while his mind dances off with his own weightless dreams.

But the currents of change still flow; the years break up and pass; and that once-young person stands before a mirror and moodily draws the tip of a finger over a crease of skin. How strange! Some little coarsening here, uncalled for, has subtly changed our familiar countenance. That childish roundness of our features is gone; the roughness of living stands out. Different thoughts swirl in the rapids of the mind, and we realize how swiftly we have been carried on through scenes and situations. School is a fading memory and, without knowing quite why, we have become a little graver, more reflective—single or married, now with children growing or with children grown, yet with our own maturity still somehow not quite accomplished; and doubt rises in us even as we tell ourselves we *ought* to be secure and capable now. The oldest generations that we remember have blown away and we find ourselves promoted to a new uncertainty. Now when a laughing group of high school or college students passes us on the sidewalk their faces and chiming voices seem—how poignant it is!—so young.

Lost in the spray and froth of time, we start to wonder about the "youth" that we thought we had. Has it in fact escaped from us, or was it always just a name and an illusion? It seems we are, incredibly, changing, going the way of our ancestors, getting older by tiny but inexorable degrees; and although we might call ourselves or others "young," "mature," "middle-aged," "elderly," we begin to realize that no category, no approximation, holds for long in this unstayable progression, this endless sloughing-off. If we stare at the hour hand of a clock we can observe no motion at all and might call out the hour as "one" or "two" or whatever; but our gaze drifts away and in a while we look up to find that the hand has sneaked into a new position and we must pronounce a new name for the time. Change goes on—has always been going on, even in the dream of childhood, even now— so if we are alert we will at length admit and ponder the fact that the concluding phase of this human life, by whatever name we call it, must be confronted soon.

What shall we make of the irreparable loss of youth and the flagging of our strength and even, perhaps, our hopes for success, triumph, vindication? In the merciless bathroom mirror the middle-aged man, lately handsome and bright, frowns at his thinning hair, his haggard look. After a party the fading beauty grows melancholy over old photographs. The athlete who yesterday was keeping up with the youngsters winces and mutters over a sore knee that somehow will not heal as quickly as it once did. Time pulls at all of us gently or sharply until we notice, and brace ourselves as we may we still give ground. We speculate about the shapeless years ahead, and doubt invades our hearts. Maybe we will not, after all, receive the recognition and thanks and praise we desire; maybe we will not get rich; maybe our dearest plans for security, long dreamed over, will not work out as we wish. In our aging parents we perceive our own destiny and, especially if we have been used to health and activity, the prospect of illness, frailty, and decline frightens us.

How can we adjust to the unstoppable slide into old age? The first thing to do is to pay attention to principles, to learn to see freshly and rebuild our view of reality. *Dukkha* or unsatisfactoriness—the elemental fire that burns living beings—must be understood profoundly in order to be escaped. Along with birth, death, sorrow, lamentation, pain, grief, and despair, the Buddha identifies old age (*jarā*) as an aspect of *dukkha*. All of us wish to live, to be—but living and being bring with them all manner of affliction. Birth ushers in aging and death. *Once* would be trouble enough, but according to Buddhism as long as craving has not been eliminated the cycle of conditioned existence keeps on turning, forcing us, in one life after another, to keep playing out the rise and fall of vitality, to keep marking the circular hours, to keep slipping from youth into age. The purpose of the Buddha's teaching is to show us how to live worthily amid these conditions and, moreover, how eventually to cast off accustomed chains and realize the sublime emancipation of *Nibbāna*.

Suppose we have some faith in the Buddhist path. Still we must suffer the same physical misfortune as other people—what about that? *Nibbāna* is hard to attain—we do not doubt it—so how are we to get along in this present life with this human body that perhaps already shows signs of deterioration? Here it helps to remember that the Buddha and his enlightened disciples themselves were not immune to the law of impermanence that slowly wrecks the body and clouds the senses, but they rejoiced in a countervailing blessing—wisdom (*paññā*). This wisdom is not a mere pile of experience or a chance spark of intuition, but rather an uncovered lamp, a timeless light revealed by the removal of obstructions from the mind. By this light perfected ones see the universe as it is and walk in confidence through perils, letting go utterly of all that causes distress or worry. Certainly they continue to feel such physical pain as the human body is liable to, but as they no longer compulsively grasp at and identify with the body its shortcomings cannot disturb their radiant peace.

Wisdom even in a lesser, modest degree is a shield against the blows of circumstance and a sustaining force amid loss and disappointment. The Buddhist way is not to ignore troubles but to probe straight into them with a contemplative mind—in fact to use those very troubles as catalysts and teachers. Are we faint-hearted? Do we lack initiative? Do we still halfway doubt the urgency of our situation or the possibility of progress? Then we should recall that the world teems with signs, portents, and legible truths. If the prospect of old age is starting to concern us—as well it should—we need not look far for "divine messengers" (*deva-dūta*) to rouse us. Indeed, we can hardly plead ignorance of their presence:

> But, my good man, did you not see among people a woman or a man aged eighty, ninety, or a hundred years, frail, bent like a roof gable, crooked, leaning on a stick, shakily going along, ailing, his youth and vigor gone, with broken teeth, with gray and scanty hair or none, wrinkled, with blotched limbs?...My good man, did it never occur to you who are intelligent and old enough, "I too am subject to old age and cannot escape it. Let me now do noble deeds by body, speech, and mind"?
>
> (Aṅguttara Nikāya III, 35)

Likewise, in a sick person we ought to recognize the divine messenger who prophesies illness, and in the dead the divine messenger solemnly reminding us of mortality and the few, precious years we may spend well or badly. A boost to our resolve can be found just in the recognition of these divine messengers all around us. Then we should take stock of our own situation and act rightly in deed, word, and thought. The Buddha teaches that all phenomena are caused and conditioned; they do not appear accidentally, but only when the necessary conditions come about. Wisdom grows up nourished by morality and concentration; thus if we need mature wisdom to defend us (and we do) we must devote ourselves to morality and concentration; in other words, we must undertake the grand path of Dhamma as shown by the Buddha.

When we were children we were given puzzle drawings, which invited us to find the little animals hidden in the grass or trees. They were there; they were certainly there all along, cunningly hidden, but we had to look closely to make out the significant figures against the deceptive background. In a similar way powerful symbols and fruitful truths constantly await our scrutiny in the tangle of daily life, but it requires a mind disciplined through morality and concentration to pick them out and comprehend them rightly. A divine messenger of old age, sickness, or death, once seen, once recognized, will step forth again and again in one guise or another, amazing us that we never noticed this visible Dhamma before. Seeing and pondering, we must exercise our newborn and still weak understanding by behaving morally and nobly, with mindfulness and energy—so that stronger understanding will be the happy result. Then it may be that when we come to deal with the wearing out of our bodies our minds will be alert and ready.

Just as in our childish ignorance we attribute permanence to the people and scenes about us, assuming they will always stay the same, so we have long been accustomed to think that wisdom, strength, ignorance, or other virtues or failings are permanent and fortuitous characteristics of people. For example, we assume that there are (somewhere) the "wise" and then there are ordinary folks like ourselves—thus we are and always will be, so why should we presume to seek insight? But this is a dreary mistake, resulting from inattention to causation and change. Wisdom does not hop out of some cosmic lottery into one person's head but not another's; rather it germinates, grows root and stalk, and bears fruit according to the efforts of the individual dedicated to his own true well-being. We cannot excuse ourselves from the religious challenge on the grounds that we are not wise, that we just do not have what it takes for enlightenment: nobody has what it takes before actually traveling the path. Even the Buddha himself, we must remember, lived innumerable lives before he reached perfection, and even in his last life he was certainly not just born into enlightenment but had to earn it. Can we in our turn respectably bemoan our lack of wisdom while refusing to cultivate it? The way, which the Buddha found and made known, lies open for us, and we can, if we will, take advantage of the opportunity just as others have done.

This is not to say that the path is short or easy, only that it is open to whoever will set out on it. What do we need to start moving? Some energy, some confidence, some inspiration born from considering the example of the Buddha, who understood and overcame mortal afflictions. Once, in the Buddha's old age, his personal attendant, Venerable Ānanda, was massaging his body, and spoke up in this way:

> It is wonderful, Lord, it is marvelous! Now the color of the Blessed One's skin is no more clear and bright: all his limbs are flaccid and wrinkled, his body is bent forward, and there seems a change in the sense faculties of his eyes, ears, nose, tongue, and bodily sensation.
> (Saṃyutta Nikāya XLVIII, 41)

Why should Venerable Ānanda find these facts wonderful or marvelous? We might reasonably guess that he saw them in the light of the Buddha's lifelong teaching about impermanence. Even the Buddha, so vigorous, vital, endowed with psychic powers, had to succumb to the decay of the body, and Venerable Ānanda was astute enough to catch the significance of the fact. If the noblest of men cannot avoid the unpleasantness of old age, then how can we? But more wonder should come from the realization that the Buddha, while deploring old age as another form of dukkha, bore his own infirmities with equanimity. The mind, we must understand, need not be a slave of the body. Radiant with wisdom and established in mindfulness, the Buddha was not upset by such a predictable, natural happening as the breaking down of his body. He had long since finished with all attachment; his mind was utterly pure, with no trace of anxiety remaining. A follower of the Buddha, reflecting on this, should see that if his own mind develops properly there will be less and less to fear about his body.

As there is a limit to the length of our lives, what may we really hope to accomplish? Or rather, what *should* we concern ourselves with right now? Most of us do not live so much in the present as *out* of the present, distractedly involved in the here and now but forever yearning, flinging imagination toward the ever-receding future. There is nothing wrong with ordinary, reasonable ambitions for our own and our family's prosperity and security—whether to start a business or build a house or learn some new skill—but it is a mistake to think that these alone, even if they work out as hoped, will ensure contentment. To live correctly, mindfully, in the present moment is to do what needs to be done now without pointless fretting about circumstances that may or may not someday come about. All we know for sure about our future is that our hand will be less steady and our eye less keen. We will someday sit as spectators while others in their youth and vigor will be raising billows of dust and winning praise. At that time will we be smiling tranquilly or grieving at loss?

Too often we use the idea of old age as a convenient storage bin for good intentions we are not willing to act upon at present, such as the intention to devote ourselves more seriously to meditation or religious study. Distractions, wants, and duties so force themselves upon the mind that only very determined people can consistently apply themselves to higher matters and remember to keep the Dhamma at the center of all their activities. Caught up in the daily fanfare, in dickering and dealing, fretting and enduring, we push off to the future–to the time when we will have least energy–those challenges that will require the most of us. We are eager enough in advancing ourselves in minor matters, and we strive honorably, it may be, to protect and support our families; we manage to extricate ourselves from many trying crises—though not from the religious one, not from the one of old age. Through the cascading years, harassed by doubts and guiltily aware of our incompleteness, we tell ourselves we are heading toward free time in the future, in retirement or old age, which we will spend, in reversal of present habit, for religious purposes. Such temporizing should make us blush, for it amounts to thinking, "Now I am too busy for the Dhamma, but when I am old and tired and can't do anything else, *then* I will see about getting enlightened." Rather than waiting for an unguaranteed future, we should practice now, using whatever time we have available, trying even in our busy hours to maintain mindfulness.

In careless people with no knowledge of the Dhamma the sight of a very old man or woman moving along slowly with the aid of a cane or a walker might evoke only indifference, or a fear of the end of enjoyments, or a perverse resolve to scratch harder for wealth, position, and pleasure while time lasts—an apt way to embitter old age when it comes. This is to ignore the divine messenger and obey the profane one. So runs the world on the rails of a desperate philosophy, but we do not have to take that train if we know a better road. We can squander our time as easily in busyness as in idleness, and no frenzies of globe-circling or empire-gathering will comfort or emancipate the baffled heart.

Life offers worthwhile employments and healthy joys, but these are not all of one kind or confined to one impermanent epoch. Might not old age become, with the right preparation, a time of ripening, of deep contemplation, of rich insight? Youth has its joys and powers, but these should not crowd out aspirations toward timeless wisdom. The young have their anguish, too, and need direction and peace. Why should they or any of us postpone indefinitely the blessings of the Dhamma when the materials for good work surround us? Birth, maturity, and death—rising, remaining, vanishing—go on succeeding one another endlessly, multitudinously, on all scales, from the explosion of stars to the twinges in our bodies to the opening and closing of wildflowers, so that we never lack themes for meditation.

The mere accumulation of years, no matter how thick with adventures, will do nothing to build up wisdom or disperse ignorance; for what is experience by itself but a disordered mass of pains and pleasures, a confusion of happenings? But when we live consciously and intently, bringing morality and concentration to bear on our experience, when we study the patterns in the tapestry of events, then we set up prime conditions for the quickening of wisdom. If death should abruptly cut off this little drama, that is beyond our power to prevent. If we should survive to an uncommon age, that is the body's business. Our business is to live now, through whatever circumstances our *kamma* provides, as clear-headed seekers of the good and the worthy.

Once the Buddha asked King Pasenadi of Kosala what he would do if he were told that a mountain as high as the sky were moving toward him from the east, inexorably crushing and destroying everything in its way, and that three other mountains were moving toward him from the west and the north and the south. The king responded:

"In such a situation, sir, a great danger of terrible destruction to human life having arisen and a human birth being so difficult to obtain, what else could be done but to practice Dhamma, to live calmly, to do good, and to make merit?"

"I tell you, O King, I put it to you: old age and death will come upon you. Since old age and death are coming, what is it you can do?"

"Since old age and death are coming upon me what else can be done but to practice Dhamma, to live calmly, to do good, and to make merit?"
(Saṃyutta Nikāya III, 3.5)

The Buddha approved of this wise answer. Indeed, those mountains of destruction are rumbling toward all of us, and our safety lies not in fluttering about but in keeping our dignity and devoting ourselves faithfully to the path. The Buddha taught that diligent practitioners of the Dhamma can bring gladness into their lives and can free themselves from suffering—can triumphantly transcend the round of birth, aging, illness, and death. How long it will take, nobody can say, but we have the comfort of knowing that the Dhamma has beneficial, calming effects that can be studied and understood right in the present moment. We do not have to look further than our own minds and bodies to avail ourselves of encouraging insight. The old, who have studied long and confirmed the Buddha's words in their own abundant experience, reap a deserved confidence. The young also, robust and smooth-browed, bless themselves when they sense the seething of change beneath all forms and begin the quest for peace. And hope belongs to those who at any age reflect on the Dhamma and turn their faces toward its heartening light.

The Buddha teaches that all phenomena of the world bear the characteristics of impermanence, unsatisfactoriness, and impersonality or nonself. Thus our fears and sorrows, even the pains of age, cannot be considered unique or lasting. Rather they can be made use of, be mined for wisdom by means of contemplation. Are we looking for instruction? Do we hope for guidance? Emblems of truth surround us. Divine messengers still visit our neighborhood. This gray hair newly discovered in our comb—how divinely it preaches! If we stand hushed for a minute out of our hectic time, we see the hair undulate and sway to our breath—gray, silver, white, catching the light and releasing it— old age tracing on air the brilliance of the Dhamma. Might it not call forth in us some gleam of insight, some bloom of confidence that a sage of times long past once saw the whole light and out of measureless compassion spoke truth?

Youth departs and age arrives. But age, too, passes, and death as well, and birth again, and the spinning of generations. We run our imagination over the great wheel and find no end. Why, if not for the sake of our freedom, did the Buddha ever open his lips and speak? Might we not get free of wheels entirely? Still we hold some life in our bodies and light in our minds. Call it youth or call it age—today is the moment when we must do what is needful.

9. Renunciation

AMONG FOLLOWERS OF THE BUDDHA there has historically been a sharp line of division between those living as householders and those who have renounced the world to take up the career of a monk or a nun. Now that Buddhism has arrived in the West and been adopted by a fair number of people, that line is sometimes called into question. Should the formal distinctions between ordained and lay people still be maintained and observed, or do new conditions require new definitions of religious vocations? What is the special meaning or value of renunciation?

The monastic or renunciative style of life was already being practiced at the time of the Buddha, and it was to this that he turned when he became disenchanted with the futile repetition of ignorance and unsatisfactoriness that everyday existence, even for a prince, seemed to entail. Seeing himself still subject to old age, sickness, and death, he could find no fulfillment in pursuing what was also subject to those conditions, so he decided to search instead for the highest good, *Nibbāna*. The disillusioned prince renounced his kingdom and undertook the ascetic way of living, determined to find a way out of all suffering.

In his journeys he encountered other ascetics, who embraced a variety of doctrines but generally shared the beliefs that life as a householder was too crowded with passions, business, and duties to allow maximum religious development, and that the surest way to enlightenment lay in simplicity, self-denial, and homelessness. These wanderers subsisted on alms, on the donations of food, clothing, medicine, and shelter given by lay people who admired them, despite their position outside of institutional religion, for their asceticism and presumed wisdom. Though their livelihood was precarious, they enjoyed a freedom from worldly responsibility that was especially advantageous for ardent seekers.

When, after years of austerities and meditation, the former prince at last achieved perfect enlightenment and became the Buddha, he did not return to the lay life but rather established and shaped the *Sangha*—the order of monks (*bhikkhus*) and later also of nuns (*bhikkhunīs*)—as a community of world-renouncing ascetics bound together both by Dhamma and by a code of discipline (*Vinaya*). His disciples were expected to avoid entanglements in the world and cherish seclusion. They were to discipline their thoughts, words, and deeds so as to apprehend the sublime truths of Dhamma for their own liberation and for the instruction of others.

The renunciative pattern had been tried and found worthy, so the Buddha carefully codified it, as occasions arose, so that those who came after him would have a clear and safe path to follow. At the same time, he taught his lay disciples the principles of good conduct that would protect them, lead them to fortunate rebirth, and lift their minds to higher teachings. These principles were not different from what he taught the monks, only on a more basic level suited to those who were unable to break with the world and undertake the way of religious homelessness. The lay life and the monastic life obviously differed in customs and outward conduct, but monks and nuns and informed lay followers were engaged in the same course of practice, the Noble Eightfold Path: right view, right intention, right speech, right action, right livelihood, right effort, right mindfulness, and right concentration.

There was no doubt that the career of renunciation was the more direct route to enlightenment, but the accomplishments of lay disciples could and sometimes did equal those of monks. We should notice, moreover, that although the Buddha lived the homeless life, he did not see the aim of the monk as an utter retreat from his fellow man.

The rules of the Sangha ensured that monks would have regular contact with the laity, if only to receive their daily alms food; and to inspire the laity to give this food the Sangha had to behave with decorum and dignity. Furthermore, the Buddha told his first fully enlightened disciples to wander abroad for the benefit and welfare of all beings—teaching the Dhamma and bringing encouragement and inspiration to the confused and unhappy.

Throughout the centuries down to our own day, the Triple Gem of Buddhism has consisted of the Buddha, the Dhamma, and the Sangha—three objects for veneration, three spiritual refuges. There are actually two kinds of Sangha, and the one meant here is the *ariyasangha*, the community of noble disciples who have attained to one or more of the stages of sainthood. There are four of these stages.

The first is that of the "stream-enterer" (*sotāpanna*), who has completely destroyed the first three of the ten fetters that bind beings to birth and death: belief in an enduring personality or self, skeptical doubt about the teaching, and attachment to rites and rituals. Because of this attainment he or she can no longer take birth in the lower, miserable planes of existence, and is assured of reaching full liberation in no more than seven future births.

The second stage is that of the "once-returner" (*sakadāgāmī*), who has succeeded in weakening greed, hatred, and delusion, and who will return to the human plane only once more before making a complete end of suffering.

The third stage is that of the "non-returner" (*anāgāmī*), who has completely broken the fourth and fifth fetters—sensuous craving and ill will—and is destined for birth in a higher plane of existence, there to achieve ultimate enlightenment.

At the fourth and highest level of attainment stands the holy one, the *arahant*, who has completed the path—realized *Nibbāna*—by breaking the last five fetters: craving for fine-material or rarefied existence, craving for immaterial existence, conceit, restlessness, and ignorance. The *arahant* lives out his or her life in serenity, and at the final breaking down of the body he or she escapes from the mental and the material entirely, going beyond all concept or imagination, free from all future birth and death.

The other kind of Sangha is the *sammuti-sangha*, the order of ordained monks and nuns, which has served as the caretaker and preserver of the teaching and—at its best—as the visible embodiment of Buddhist ideals. The ordination lineage of *Theravāda* Buddhist nuns was lost many centuries ago for unknown reasons, but there exist today communities of modern *Theravāda* nuns who follow eight or ten basic rules. The ordination lineage of monks, meanwhile, has survived to the present day, and branches of it are to be found throughout the world. Monks must follow 227 basic precepts of morality and proper monastic conduct, along with numerous rules and procedures for the maintenance of their communal life. They are expected to put into practice the original doctrine of the Buddha through their own renunciation, study, and meditation.

Nowadays the usefulness of this Sangha might be questioned. "Is it really necessary to leave the world?" we might wonder. "Can't we practice the Dhamma as lay people and householders without all the formality and restrictions that monks undergo, without renouncing so much?"

Is it really necessary to leave the world? That depends on what we want to accomplish and how intensively we want to practice. If we wish to live a virtuous life, train our minds, and lay the groundwork for happy future lives, no, it is not absolutely necessary. An unfortunate, incorrect view, still widespread among Buddhists, is that only monks or exceptionally inspired lay people can or should practice meditation and attain great insight. On the contrary, the Dhamma, including the higher reaches of meditation, is available to and practicable by all, whatever their situation. Whoever makes intelligent effort can gain the benefits of clear-mindedness and equanimity. This cannot be emphasized enough. But it is also true that if one wishes to strive exclusively for liberation from *saṃsāra* and has sufficient conviction and opportunity, the best path remains that of renunciation. Though lay people can reach stages of sainthood, such success is especially difficult because the routine of a lay person overflows with distractions, worries, and mundane duties that make it hard to keep up steady *bhāvanā*, or mental development.

Buddhism certainly does not require anyone to renounce the world entirely; rather, those who follow Buddhism with the aim of reducing present suffering may find that they are led naturally and gradually to more and more simplicity and renunciation in their everyday affairs. If they should go far enough, the homeless, monastic life might begin to attract them. The world of commerce and social interchange forever shudders with craving and aversion, with making, doing, dealing, and acquiring; it has little room or understanding for quietude, silence, and cessation of passions—hence the need for the refuge offered by the Sangha. It is possible to live an ascetic, meditative life as a lay person—and this is a praiseworthy thing—but usually one will still have to work at a job and stay involved in the business of lay society in many ways. And aside from material concerns the Sangha offers invaluable tradition, teaching, discipline, and communal support to the practitioner. The rules and formalities of the Sangha, which seem daunting at first, actually promote polite social relations, freedom from remorse, and the orderly functioning of the order as a whole.

To the lay Buddhist the Sangha gives inspiration, instruction, and the opportunity to make merit through acts of faith and generosity. The sight of a well-practicing order—behaving with dignity, restraint, and grace, intent on the training—lifts the heart and inspires confidence. Here is a visible fruit of the Buddha's word—still alive and fresh after all these centuries, still offering the precious Dhamma to cure the sickness of the world. Good, mature monks have not only studied the Dhamma but have spent years testing it and living in accordance with it, and can teach with an authority and an impact that books cannot equal. The layman can listen, ask questions, present problems, get advice, and learn how to meet troubles with the aid of Dhamma.

As a materially dependent community, the Sangha gives the laity the chance to practice the primary virtue of giving. Although one's time might be consumed by work and family duties, although one might not be prepared to undertake systematic study or strict meditation oneself, one can still offer food or medicine or other necessities to those who have embarked on the monastic career. Such giving is a forthright and concrete act, deeply satisfying, bringing immediate gladness, and bringing future gladness, too.

In their relations with the Sangha the lay people, through their generosity, faith, moral restraint, and meditative effort, effectively protect and advance the whole *sāsana*—the Buddhist religion in its wide dimensions. In respecting and encouraging renunciation in others, one strengthens wholesome aspirations in oneself. Seeing good discipline, one is moved to emulate it. Hearing deep teaching, one forms the intention to experience it. Observing devotion, one looks to cultivate it within oneself. So it is that the formal renunciation of a relatively small number benefits many others and raises enlightenment as an ideal and an inspiration for all.

Many Buddhists in recent years have tried to reconcile somewhat the social, everyday world and the path to enlightenment, reasoning correctly that the practice of meditation does not absolutely require silence or solitude or escape from society, and that practitioners can make genuine progress while living as householders in the midst of lay society. In this there arises no contradiction to ancient tradition. Indeed, the appearance of lay meditation centers and the popularity of meditation courses are encouraging signs that the Dhamma is being taken seriously. But it would be wrong to assume that a few weekends or weeks of meditation each year—though these are fine accomplishments—are all that anyone can or should do to reach enlightenment. Individuals differ in their spiritual interests, intentions, and energies. In any case, a meditatively inclined person must be prepared to recognize and discard bad habits, and to realize that the good work will not be completed until the mind is fully purified.

If we are new explorers of Buddhism we might find much attraction in its meditation techniques but rather less in those aspects of the Dhamma that run against the current of the world—such as advice to restrain the senses, to refrain from immoral conduct, and to avoid dissipating amusements. We indeed want enlightenment, as long as the practice does not interfere too much with our established preferences. There is nothing very surprising about this partial approach to Buddhism, given the fragmentary and sometimes contradictory hunks of information that we might pick up. For the moment, relatively few monks are to be found in the West. Without experienced, qualified monks (never in abundance) as teachers and models of formal renunciation, and without a revered body of community and family tradition to learn from, we may, in our solitary investigations, get inaccurate ideas of what Buddhist monasticism is all about and what the advantages are of a formal system of self-discipline in religious practice.

Buddhist monasticism as a living institution being so little known to society in the West, we might at first tend to view the Sangha as unimportant to religious life, or see formal commitment to a monastic order as disagreeably restrictive, or regard monks' rules as obsolete or outmoded. Modern industrial society promotes ideals of busyness and intense involvement in social affairs, so the monastic ideal of renunciation and uninvolvement appears very odd. The religious renouncer, who gladly consents to live under rules for his own betterment, might be seen as a gloomy fellow who incomprehensibly cuts himself off from the wonderful pleasures of life. Human beings are generally intent on enjoying things, and a doctrine that questions this enjoyment arouses puzzlement and discomfort in our minds, making it difficult to discern the plain and frugal path of life that leads to true happiness.

But we cannot thoughtlessly indulge ourselves and climb spiritual peaks at the same time, because the pursuit of pleasure weakens the self-restraint that is necessary for progress toward wisdom. While many pleasant, interesting, and agreeable things are to be found in the world, infatuation with them turns the individual away from the path of striving and in the long run ensures the repetition of suffering. The renouncer, whether an ordained monk or simply a lay practitioner who withdraws to some extent from the cacophony of society, does not want to experience an infinite string of empty excitements. It is not that he or she is unconscious of beauty or unaffected by pleasure, but that he or she suspects their inadequacy and hindering effect. Moreover, much of what people take to be pleasure is in fact suffering with a sugary coating, which deceives and poisons the unwary. One remarkable aspect of Buddhist teaching, therefore, is that what we need to do is not to stuff ourselves with tasty experiences, not to acquire things, but rather to get free of them, to get rid of attachment, aversion, delusion, to discard the preoccupations, opinions, and defilements that prevent us from seeing things clearly. Renunciation helps us to accomplish this, even through the relatively simple rejection of excessive possessions, diversions, and entertainments under whose weight we have struggled so long.

Renunciation begins in the midst of the householder's life with a thoughtful avoidance of superfluous objects, appetites, and activities, and develops naturally and gradually as one perceives the benefits of simplicity. How many of the possessions we surround ourselves with are really essential to our well-being? Would a new vacation house or automobile or sailboat really bring more satisfaction than trouble? Could a voluntary reduction in the number of our appointments, meetings, shows, and parties ease our minds a bit? Perhaps we could turn the television set off for an hour and meditate. Perhaps we could refrain from alcohol and intoxicating drugs and meet anxiety with mindfulness instead. Perhaps we do not really need, or even enjoy, all we think we do. To be sure, there is delight and satisfaction to be found in the worldly life, and each person has to decide for himself what degree of activity is suitable for him and how far he wants to seek the quite different and higher satisfaction of renunciation.

Because we harbor restless, conflicting ideas and feelings, we might both shun and admire the life of renunciation. Treasuring our attachments to possessions and amusements, we shrink from the idea of actually giving them up as from something oppressive and frightening. The existence of a few diligent, ascetic practitioners provides a troubling contrast to this familiar sphere of material preoccupations, and calls up confused emotions. It is tempting to dismiss the Sangha as irrelevant or unnecessary. In these exciting modern days renunciation and adherence to an ancient discipline might seem absurd and contrary to our cultural standards of self-expression and exuberant external activity. But at the same time, thoughtful people remain respectful of renunciation and of those few who give up so much in pursuit of liberation. We may read stories of hermits and ascetics and their years of sacrifice and lonely struggle, and these may well appeal to our religious imagination; and to see or to meet those who actually devote themselves to that strenuous life of striving can be undeniably inspiring. Even in the monastic Sangha there are not many such persons, but they do exist. Those who renounce the world in this way may be useless to the material ends of society, and yet, in service to a higher purpose, they carry on and keep alive the purest hopes of humanity.

The Buddha renounced the world to go in search of enlightenment and, having found it, *stayed* out of the circle of worldly society, having no wish to recover his position as a prince or to settle down in a domestic fashion. This is a very significant fact, often overlooked. It indicates, first, what everyone probably suspects—that mundane preoccupations tend to cramp the religious impulse and, second, that renunciation opens the way to happiness and freedom superior to the ordinary kinds. Still, in the Buddha's case, as probably in all human cases, the crucial renunciation is the mental one—the determined effort to get rid of wrong views and wrong habits—not merely the physical act of taking to the woods.

Many people of conventional opinions probably look on renunciation for religious purposes as a bizarre rejection of valuable opportunities in life; others of romantic temperament dream about being a saintly wanderer with an alms bowl, beatifically meditating in scenic spots with good weather. Both sorts misunderstand renunciation, which is a rational discipline, a kind of work that begins with the thoughtful householder and reaches its fulfillment not in the external dress of a monk or a nun, but in the mind purified and exalted by wisdom.

Even for confirmed Buddhists ambivalence toward renunciation is not likely to disappear soon. Part of it depends on the capricious nature of the mind, and part depends on the character of the renouncing persons one knows or hears about. Those who strive toward the ideals of the Sangha, keeping the rules, patiently following in the footsteps of the Buddha regardless of admiration or blame, tend to earn respect and confidence. Though we cannot help but be profoundly influenced by individuals we meet—both the good and the bad—we would do well to temper our enthusiasms and disappointments by remembering that few Buddhists, even few renouncers, consistently live up to the highest standards.

The difficulty of the direct path to enlightenment, however, is no reason to dismiss and deny it, even if we ourselves are not prepared to follow it. We ought not to lull ourselves by thinking that we might be able to live simultaneously in the world and out of it—perfectly enlightened yet avidly pursuing worldly pleasures. We should rather recognize where we stand and try to make the most out of our circumstances, keeping Buddhist ideals before our minds even as we carry out our ordinary duties.

Ultimately, the difference between Sangha and laity must be recognized because it exists in fact as well as in theory: most Buddhists remain tied to the world while some have cut their formal ties. The cutting of the other ties, the ties of craving and clinging, is the duty of both monk and layman, and in this sense both kinds of Buddhists are or should be engaged in a religious vocation. But the ancient institution of the Sangha is pledged and best equipped to carry out the full requirements of the Dhamma. Because human life is short, and because a Buddha appears only rarely to rediscover and teach the way to deliverance, and because no one has a guarantee of opportunities to learn and practice Dhamma in the future, there is no time to be lost, and for those who are truly prepared and determined the course of monastic renunciation remains open.

The *sammuti-sangha*, the ordinary, mundane Sangha, which is large and diverse and far from perfect, does not constitute the ultimate refuge; it only grants the means, the discipline, the framework for the efforts of ardent pilgrims. The monastic path is a unique way of life that reaches quite beyond temporal satisfactions, but it is not something that everyone will find possible, and the Buddha surely had no expectation that his listeners would leave their trades and homes en masse to become religious mendicants. He taught the Dhamma because he knew it would be for the happiness and welfare of all persons who paid attention. He established the Sangha to serve as the immediate vehicle for some and the inspiring beacon for others. While the great majority of Buddhists have preferred to remain lay persons, the continued existence of this Sangha, and particularly of the small vanguard within it, reminds us of the beneficent Dhamma and points to *Nibbāna*, our common goal, the release from our long travail.

The enthusiasm nowadays for serious books on Dhamma, meditation courses, and religious retreats indicates the wish of many lay people to practice almost monastically for greater or lesser periods of time. It suggests that, despite the frivolity of our society and our own weaknesses, many of us do respect the ideals of simplicity, celibacy, and mental striving, and want to approach them as near as we can. As Buddhism grows in the modern world, along with it has grown, quietly, an interest in more organized religious life, scriptural study, and systematic meditation practice. Over time such interest should ripen into the realization that the monastic Sangha is integral to the religious life of Buddhist families and individuals. We need the warm sense of being connected through faith and graceful tradition to the compassionate sage, the supremely enlightened Buddha. We need, for our own health and peace, the inspiration and the gladness that come from respecting that which is worthy of respect. When we turn from hopeful imagination to the beaten-down, dispirited world, when we think, with dimming smile, of the hard work ahead of us in combatting craving, it is reassuring to know and to see that the institution into which the Buddha put his labor and his teaching remains alive, that the good discipline is not forgotten, that renunciation and simplicity can still be practiced.

Where there is the resolve to renounce what should be renounced, even in modest ways, there is the possibility of real progress toward freedom. If we practice the Dhamma faithfully right now in the household life, making use of opportunities as they appear, we will find ourselves better able to cope with the world as it is, to avoid its dangers, and to establish ourselves on a good course. But whatever external circumstances may provide, our important duty is just to keep training and developing our own minds. All grasping is affliction. Tight and trembling though our thoughts may be, they need not stay so. We might yet, by mindful degrees, relax the baneful tension, let go of sorrow, renounce unworthy deeds, and discard the burdens of defilement until the grave weight is gone and our hands at last are empty—and free.

10. *The Life of Honor*

🌿 To LIVE AS BUDDHISTS, to apply Buddhist principles beneficially to daily affairs, we need to observe specific points of moral discipline—and more. It is right for us to take care in following moral precepts and actively sympathizing with other living beings, but occasional grains of virtue dropped on the earth do not by themselves build up an enduring, noble character. There must be consistency in our work; there must also be a mortar of understanding, a will to bind the elements, and a faith in the beauty of the outcome. Buddhism teaches that human beings are imperfect yet may become perfect by their own exertions, as long as those exertions are directed along the Noble Eightfold Path.

In weighing our choices and distinguishing our duties in the hurly-burly of professional, social, and family life, we do well to remember honor—a sense of consistent integrity and devotion to right principles. The honorable man or woman is aware of his or her own spiritual growth, of how that growth might be stimulated, and conversely of how that growth might be slowed or reversed by impure actions. One who is intent on his own welfare and the welfare of others should continually look at himself with mindfulness and reflect on his own shortcomings and his rightful tasks still not completed.

There is no one, the Buddha said, who does not hold himself dearer than anyone else in the world; yet in taking care of ourselves and wishing ourselves well we are faced with a practical problem because simple gratification of our desires—the most obvious course—is not always possible and, anyway, does not make us happy but rather tends to degrade us to acquisitiveness and frustration. To keep a calm mind and a resilient heart we must in all our dealings with nature and society be honorable; that is, we must be mindful of and faithful to that which is true and worthy—namely, the Dhamma. Honor consists not just in carefully applying virtue or morality (*sīla*) to all situations, but also in understanding and appreciating the ideal human beings we might become. This personal honor, an adopted standard independent of the praise or blame that society assigns, can sustain and console us through troubles, especially as what the world or our companions call good may not be so.

What do we do in doubtful circumstances when we cannot call an explicit precept to mind or, if we can, are not sure how it might apply? How do we react when our companions behave badly or questionably and wish us to join them? Do we go along with the general will or detach ourselves from the proceedings? Let us think what might happen when our business or social dealings bring us into contact with those less scrupulous than we think ourselves to be. Suppose someone suggests gaining an advantage through some slight obscuring of the truth. Perhaps a promise could be made with no intention of fulfilling it. Or suppose we consider withholding from a customer important information during a sale. Or maybe it is possible to rephrase a business report to distort the reality of a situation. Nobody proposes outright lies or theft, perhaps, yet a sensitive person might worry that affairs are drifting toward the unethical. While everybody professes belief in ethical behavior, such belief likely amounts to very little unless backed by practical judgment, reverence for moral precepts, and a sense of honor.

When the stain of dishonesty seeps into our business or social affairs or any activity, we would be wise to identify it and wipe it away at once, if possible, or to disassociate ourselves from the ugly environment. But under the pressure of circumstances and others' opinions we might waver and rationalize and bend more than we would like in order not to give offense or become unpopular. So potent is the will of a group that, with troubled conscience, we might be cowed into going along with what we hope is a minor and temporary evil. But each little retreat from principles, lamentably, makes the force of expediency harder to resist and mental development harder to accomplish.

Honor can prevent such enfeebling retreats because it gives us an ideal more precious than the opinion of our fellows. We can then disagree and withhold our consent when necessary because rejecting duplicity and dishonesty means heeding our own best aspirations, confirming our commitment to virtue. Seen in this light, even an awkward situation can become an occasion for self-improvement. Even though a particular course of action might not seem entirely or technically immoral, if it provokes worrisome doubts or makes us feel uncomfortably close to error we do wisely not to follow it, because we value our personal honor. Thus, by abstaining or turning to a nobler course, we give force and reality to that honor.

Business, family life, social relations—no sphere of action escapes ambiguities; and we are daily tempted, urged, pushed toward deeds of doubtful quality. Mostly these do not involve complicity with others but concern our desires and conscience only. Take the matter of petty pilfering. Suppose we are tempted to take without permission some items belonging to our place of work and not return them— miscellaneous supplies, tools, gadgets, appliances, etc. Our employer, we might reason, is rich, and underpays us, and anyway will not miss the articles in question. These arguments conceivably could all be true, but would they really change the nature of our taking? Would we remove such articles openly, or would we feel it necessary to conceal them? This is a telling point, worth examining. Secretiveness should be an alarm bell for the conscience.

Desires will move us precipitately if we let them, if we do not take a moment to remember our principles. How do we act, for instance, if our car hits and damages a parked car when its owner is nowhere to be seen? It would be very easy just to drive away. Should we? What does honor say? The sort of conduct we would condemn in others will not look any better in us. All of us have conflicting instincts for the noble and the ignoble that bend our thoughts, and that may be heeded or disregarded, as we choose. Before we let nimble rationalizations dispose of a problem we ought to attend to the clash of desire and principle that goes on underneath, so that we can name our motives plainly and act out of wisdom rather than habit.

The mind, as we know, is slippery and subtle, so when we find it hard to reason point by point through a problem it helps to ask ourselves: Is this what an honorable person would do? Is this consistent with Buddhist principles? Will this act cause harm or benefit for others? Will it injure or protect my sense of honor and self-respect? Because every person considers his or her own welfare before all else, such reflections can encourage us to act rightly.

Buddhism teaches that intentional action—*kamma*—has consequences for the doer, in this present life or the next life or some future life beyond that. This is the practical basis of Buddhist moral discipline. If a deed is bad by its nature—if it erupts from the depths of greed, hatred, or delusion—then its effect upon the doer will tend to be equivalently bad, irrespective of his rationalizations. We must understand that mere opinions and self-justifying theories do not offset the results of our intentional, willful deeds by body, speech, or mind, which come to us sooner or later in the form of fortune or misfortune. We might tell ourselves that we are justified in committing a certain action—we might even enjoy the stout approval of our friends—but the true root of the action, wholesome or unwholesome, whether recognized or not, is what determines its potential for result.

We are responsible for our own deeds and we will receive the due results of those deeds; and understanding this fact is an important part of right view. But this process of *kamma* should not be taken as any kind of rigid fate. We cannot predict that a particular deed will have just a particular outcome in the future, because conditions are constantly shifting and because we are always performing fresh actions of varying quality that continually modify the stream of our existence. Therefore if we suffer regret and guilt over some wrong deed we have done, the right course is to resolve firmly not to act that way again and to devote ourselves more seriously to performing good and meritorious actions. The more good we perform, the cleaner the stream will flow.

Virtue is an unfailing investment and protection, and we should pay attention to the volitional actions that will work for our merit over time, and worry less about the disadvantages of acting according to morality here and now. For it is true that by keeping moral rules we will sometimes incur hardships—it may very well cost us something to behave honorably. Other people may object to our interpretations of integrity and fair dealing, and personal relationships and jobs may become more difficult. Especially in times of hurry and pressure we might be tempted to relax our discipline, finding it hard to carry on when we can see much vexation and no immediate advantage. But just as a muscle grows strong with exercise, so health of mind increases when we act against difficulty and overcome it. Then, subtly perhaps, we experience a sense of accomplishment that nourishes our further efforts to progress in the Dhamma.

To adhere faithfully to the principles of the Noble Eightfold Path is not easy, but the existence, even within our own circle of acquaintance, perhaps, of a few fine people who give up personal advantage for honor should convince us that spiritual progress is not impossible but within reach of those who will take moral discipline seriously and not despair at the first obstacle. Clearly this requires individual initiative, as society at large tends toward expediency and sometimes distrusts those who stand out through uprightness, even though it may not be their wish to stand out at all but only to obey higher principles.

What society labels as good or evil may or may not be so. Intentions and results must be examined strictly. We must be alert to who suffers, who benefits, and what we really intend beneath our protestations and decisions and actions—not relying casually on apparent public opinion as our teacher, not trying to pass off moral responsibility to others. The times change and fashions change, obliging the honorable person to seek always for principle beneath the fluctuations of circumstance. Our society increasingly condones, for example, euthanasia for very ill or debilitated people—a form of intentional killing that is definitely contrary to Buddhist teaching and whose seriousness is not at all diminished by the approval of the few or the many. What changes over time is not the essential quality of deeds but the species of public delusion. To live a life of honor is to examine and to act on the basis of timeless Dhamma, which is universally beneficial and altogether superior to the rationalizations of the day.

In order to distinguish good from evil, to act upon the good, and to make progress toward enlightenment, we need to make use of all the factors of the Noble Eightfold Path, not just a selected few. The path can be divided into three groups: morality, concentration, and wisdom. The morality group consists of right speech, right action, and right livelihood. The concentration group consists of right effort, right mindfulness, and right concentration. The wisdom group consists of right view and right intention. The three groups and the eight factors support each other; they do not stand isolated; they are to be practiced together to put an end to suffering. In order to do this work we need to maintain a clear conscience; in order to obtain that we must stop doing unwholesome and evil actions. This means, as a prerequisite, restraining ourselves by moral rules.

But why, we might wonder, must we concern ourselves with mere rules? Shouldn't sincerity and good intentions be sufficient? Are we living just to be able to check off technical points on a list? Truly, Buddhist morality should not be a perfunctory operation but a wakeful recognition of and respect for those qualities that actually help us and help others. But until we can attain enlightenment our understanding will remain incomplete and subject to error, so we require explicit guidance from someone wiser than we are. The basic five precepts, which the Buddhist layman voluntarily undertakes out of confidence, are vital guideposts or boundary markers on the road to liberation. By refraining from killing, refraining from taking what is not given or stealing, refraining from sexual misconduct, refraining from false speech, and refraining from taking intoxicants, one gains safety and keeps to the open track where progress is possible.

By refraining from killing, the practitioner benefits himself in two ways: he avoids the effects of the bad *kamma* of causing injury and death to others, and he stimulates in himself the growth of compassion. Not killing, not taking life, means exactly that. The precept does not apply just to human beings but to animals as well, small or large, loved or unloved. The strict follower of this precept does not kill for food, for sport, for enmity, or for any other reason.

It might be objected that in a world crowded with human beings and animals getting in each other's way, it is inconvenient and difficult to keep this precept. Certainly this is true—all the precepts are inconvenient; all moral discipline requires control of our natural urges, because those urges so often inflict harm on others and on ourselves. Deeds of willful killing and harming vary in their moral weight according to various factors such as the nature of the injury, the characteristics of the victim, and the intentions of the doer of the deeds; but such deeds are all unwholesome and liable to produce bad results in the future. To abstain from killing and harming entails a healthy recognition of our freedom and responsibility in making a happy future. It requires effort, and the more conscientious that effort is, the better it will be for us and for all creatures around us. There may come a time when *we* will sorely need compassion.

The precept against taking what is not given applies not only to blatant theft or robbery but also to all forms of dishonestly taking others' money or property. It includes all kinds of wrongful acquisition of what does not belong to oneself, whether accomplished by deceit, fraud, intimidation, or other means. Breaking into a house and carrying off the furniture is obviously theft, but so also is cheating a business customer or supplier out of a few dollars or a few cents. Borrowing with no intention of paying back, falsifying expense account reports, embezzling—all these and many more are reprehensible acts violating the principle of not stealing. Thus the precept, when broadly applied, will not only forestall obvious legal and social trouble but will also defend against corrupting tendencies and bolster one's sense of honor and respect for the ideals of purity and innocence. Moreover, reverence for this precept naturally finds expression in the outwardly directed virtue of giving (*dāna*). Not only does the carefully practicing Buddhist refrain from taking what is not his, but he becomes more willing to bestow gifts and kindnesses on others. The precept, consciously applied, curbs selfishness and encourages the cultivation of wholesome and morally beneficial action.

The precept against sexual misconduct likewise has wide applications and benefits. The Buddha realistically understood the sexual drive as a particularly powerful form of craving and did not try either to deny its force or to romanticize it. Like all passions, it impedes meditation and the attainment of equanimity; it inflames and upsets the mind. Clearly it is inconsistent with a career of renunciation; thus monks and nuns must train themselves in celibacy; and devout lay people as well have traditionally abstained from sexual indulgence on religious holidays and during periods of intensive meditation.

For the layman, absorbed in the business of the world, the Buddha recommended a firm and realistic standard of discipline in sexual matters. Basically, refraining from sexual misconduct means refraining from adultery, unfaithfulness, and sexual license. It entails never committing deeds of sexual coercion, seduction, molestation, or other such indecent behavior. One who heeds this precept has no sexual relations with unsuitable persons; that is, with the wives or husbands of others, with engaged or betrothed persons, with children, with any helpless or unwilling parties, or with anyone else not competent or free to reject sexual attentions.

Sexual relationships between independent, unmarried people, provided they do not violate any of these points, are not prohibited by the precept—although it is good to remember that heedless sexual indulgence leads to many sorts of misery and that desire by itself is not a reliable guide to what is good and suitable. A thoughtful reserve in sexual matters will do much to prevent future regret and will preserve integrity and self-respect. It will also promote the balance and calm so important in Buddhist practice.

Refraining from false speech has applications beyond avoidance of gross lying. This precept, together with the principles of right speech, the third factor of the Noble Eightfold Path, requires a dedication to fair and mild speech and an avoidance of all kinds of speech expressing ill will, foolishness, and deception. Specifically, the practitioner must avoid lying in all its forms; but also, taking into account the broader principles of right speech, he or she should abstain from slanderous speech, abusive speech, and pointless, silly chatter. Taken seriously, this discipline helps to strengthen mindfulness, solidify friendships, establish a good reputation, and awaken an appreciation of judicious speech such as the Buddha himself employed and recommended.

The fifth precept, refraining from taking alcoholic drinks and intoxicants that blur the mind, seems at first glance of minor significance, unrelated to weighty moral matters. Provided it is not carried too far, we might wonder, what is wrong with drinking? This precept deserves respect because it defends the other precepts and specifically guards against attacks of deluded thinking. Alcohol and other mind-blurring drugs push away inhibitions, sabotage self-control, damage reputations, ruin health, and distort mental functions. Destructive craving and aversion can thus break out more easily in speech and action. Since the practice of Dhamma demands self-restraint and clear sight, it is good to respect this precept and abstain from intoxicating, mind-unbalancing drinks, drugs, chemicals, etc. Like the other precepts, this one has a positive effect on those who honor it: it encourages and strengthens the larger effort to overcome delusion, to confront life exactly as it is with mindfulness.

Taken together, these five basic precepts of the lay Buddhist mark out the boundaries of safe conduct and set up the foundations for an honorable life. In order to abide by these precepts we need, in addition to an intellectual understanding of their importance, a way of dealing with our own weaknesses. The Buddha says that control of the senses is the basis for morality—the practical means by which we can avoid trouble and keep our resolutions. When we give unwise attention here and there, tarrying in tempting atmospheres, dwelling incautiously on the allure or repulsiveness of objects and ideas, we give craving or aversion or delusion a chance to boil up and overwhelm us. Thus we should break the power of troubling sensations by regarding them with sharp mindfulness or by avoiding them altogether. Recognizing a weakness for lust, we should stay away from titillating entertainments. Recognizing a tendency toward anger, we should not put ourselves in a position to exchange provoking words. Recognizing a liability to confusion and delusion, we should keep away from bad companions and not suffer their influences. It is simple prudence to walk out of range of temptation.

Besides the careful avoidance of harmful courses of action, we should develop the four "divine abodes" of loving kindness, compassion, sympathetic joy, and equanimity, until our morality, our *sīla*, becomes mindful, undeviating, and natural. What begins as self-discipline eventually becomes self-transcendence. By restraining our unwholesome tendencies we make possible the growth of wholesome tendencies, just as when weeds are pulled flowers have room to grow. When we keep the precepts faithfully, even when it is very difficult to do so, we prevent the start of many unruly chains of errors; the mind becomes lighter, less subject to guilt and fear. Having a quieter con-science, not being preoccupied with fear of possible results of bad deeds, we become increasingly sensitive to the suffering of our fellow creatures, careful not to harm them, solicitous for their welfare.

For our own happiness and for the happiness of others we should fulfill certain social obligations—certain practical religious duties. The Buddha sees these in terms of important relationships between chil-dren and parents, teachers and pupils, wives and husbands, friends and friends, employers and employees, religious mendicants and house-holders. For families and society to prosper these relationships should be based on mutual kindness and reciprocal responsibilities. Children should revere and support their parents. Parents should instruct and guard their children and provide for their futures. The student should learn his lessons well and attend on his teacher with respect. The teacher should take an interest in the student, seeing to his well-being in addition to his education. Wives and husbands should be faithful to one another, protecting the family wealth, doing their work with good will. Friends should treat each other with generosity, kindness, and courtesy; also they should comfort and protect one another when misfortunes come. Employers should see to the welfare of their employees by allotting work, wages, and benefits fairly and remem-bering to give bonuses from time to time. Employees in turn should honestly and diligently carry out their tasks. The householder should act kindly toward those who have undertaken the mendicant religious career, supplying them with the necessities of life; and they, for their part, should instruct and guide the householder in beneficial principles that lead to happiness here and in future lives.

The Buddha says that in protecting oneself one protects others, and in protecting others one protects oneself. A notable quality of honor-able people, who have taken this wisdom to heart, is their willingness to act contrary to immediate self-interest, to forgo profit, or even to accept loss in devotion to a higher ideal. The slack and the dull do not understand how someone might pass up a quick dollar that is a little bit tainted, or take on a responsibility that could be easily shirked, or choose moral principle over material gain. The attentive, however, have another way of seeing, and realize that principle is the most concrete thing in the impermanent universe—that which can be relied on when mundane provisions run out.

An honorable person remains quite aware of his or her own interest, but views it with deliberation and gives thought to the future effects of present deeds, remembering that future blessings will result from following good standards now. For example, consider the situation of a woman who finds herself inconveniently and unhappily pregnant. When confidence in Buddhist principles has not been firmly established, confusion and fear might dominate the mind, making abortion seem an acceptable option. Nowadays millions of women, perhaps over their private qualms, decide to undergo this procedure, the details of which few probably would wish to contemplate closely. But is it moral or honorable? Unquestionably it is contrary to the first precept—to refrain from killing. Taking the life of a human being in the womb seriously violates the moral principle and cannot be disguised by euphemisms. One knows one's intention, though not where it might lead, not what the repercussions might be. To carry out this act, or to have it carried out, is to turn away grievously, unwisely, from the path of benevolence. Intentional action—*kamma*—has consequences for the doer, irrespective of his or her preferences, according to the quality of the action; therefore mildness and mercy will promote future well-being and great advantage, while the taking of life, even for seemingly convincing reasons, will increase suffering.

The functioning of *kamma* is an unconscious process of nature whereby deeds give rise to appropriate results in the way that a planted seed naturally gives rise to a certain kind of fruit. Bearing this in mind, and bearing in mind the sweet, spreading compassion that is the very fragrance of the Dhamma, one who is really intent on future welfare should generate harmless, peaceful, kind thoughts, and accept with fortitude the undesired—and temporary—condition of unwelcome pregnancy, and thereby take a step toward real security and happiness.

A wise heart is one that listens, not to the clangor of passion and the din of ego, but to the calm and calming voice of Dhamma, which speaks out of the silence of mindful contemplation. What self is here that must be indulged, that must take offense, defend territory, or revenge injuries? Real honor cannot be sullied by another and thus cannot justify fury and vengeance. It consists in love of the good and reverence for the noble being we might someday become: the *ariya-puggala*, the noble person whose nobility comes not from birth or station but from worthy deeds and pure thoughts. The natural ally of honor is thus not pride—a defilement that shackles and corrupts the mind—but humility, the understanding that because we are not perfect and because the jungle of *saṃsāra* is full of danger we must strive to find safety in the cultivation of virtue and wisdom.

Because circumstances continually change, we cannot predict our future and must behave with becoming modesty so that we may earn release from suffering someday. We should calmly recognize the wrongs we have done—neither excusing ourselves nor indulging in useless self-castigation and pessimism—and make sure we do not repeat them. Every day offers us fresh chances to redirect our lives through conscious, wholesome actions of body, speech, and mind. All of us have, through the infinity of past time, performed innumerable good and bad deeds that variously influence the restless, running stream of our being. Whatever our regrets over past offenses, we can always carry on the noble and immediate work of purification, letting fresh springs of clean water gush in to bathe and soothe us. Having observed and pondered the causes and effects of deeds, we should be ever zealous in doing good deeds, knowing that the accumulation of these certainly will work out to our own happiness in the future.

Awareness of our own errors should help us to prevent the build-up of conceit and to become more understanding of the errors of others. Countless living beings stumble in the darkness of *saṃsāra*—and we among them. Awareness of the virtues of others, in addition, will shine an edifying light on our own problems. We are not the only ones longing for the good, and quiet, inspiring examples of honor and nobility can be seen all around us.

Honor does not require of us a bellicose objection to the actions of others. If the vote goes against us, if our opinions are discounted, if we fail to get our way, we are not thereby entitled to behave like spoiled children; rather we should keep as much dignity and poise when we are thwarted as when we are accommodated. We cannot win all contests, and we cannot expect that the world will conform to our personal moral vision. We should seek concord always and compromise when we can; but we must see the limits of compromise and go the way of Dhamma quietly, even alone, even if that ruffles others.

By safeguarding our honor we may gain a justified reputation as trustworthy people of upright character, which will make it easier for us to get along in the complexities of daily life. By attention to honor we can bring our own best thoughts of charity and generosity through to action, giving ourselves and others cause for gladness. Moreover, we can enjoy the peace of knowing that, even if only in small ways, we have beaten back unworthy intentions, held our faith, and advanced in virtue.

But beyond these benefits, honor is precious because, consciously or not, we are daily adding to a stream of actions—of *kamma*—that will be our support and that will mark our future. The Buddha teaches us that our own deeds will be our inheritance and our refuge. They should therefore be such that we can live on and die on with a tranquil mind. By raising up a sense of honor we begin to lift our ideals and the trend of our habitual conduct from the level of perishing material to the higher, finer plane where the holy ones have stood— and where we too might someday stand.

11. *A Glimpse of a Crane*

🍂 Seen through a window as our bus rounds a curve, a crane flaps into the air above misty fields. Its wings flash splendidly in the morning light and its body seems correspondingly to dwindle as it catches the rhythm of its kind and sails higher in gray-green space. A brief moment of thoughtless grace—but not one we should swallow whole out of hunger for beauty. There is more there than color and motion, more to be apprehended mindfully. Look how grand and sure those white wings are, how trivial, by comparison, the meager body they transport. What carries what? Does the bird own the wings or the wings the bird?

Though the crane does not care for philosophy we must, for we see what it does not: that it will end as offal in a field or thicket, defunct and forgotten, in its time having only flown some instinctive patterns and perhaps hatched some broods of young. But now it hatches pleasure and perplexity in the mind of a watcher. Nature imbues such energy, grace, and beauty in creatures who will come to nothing; it launches them splendidly in an upward arc, then lets them fall, to scatter their offspring who will helplessly run through the same picturesque and troubling sequence.

The individual creature scarcely matters to nature—observers have long realized this. But deeper reflection tells us that the species as well scarcely matters. What nature cares for—if we can personify it for a moment—is no particular class or individual but only the throb of cause and effect, only a reflexive continuity, a pulsation of appetite and growth expressed through a multitude of forms. In this cycle without end the crane serves the wings and the wings serve the crane; and wings and body of the laboring animal exert themselves ultimately in the service of *taṇhā*, craving, the primal obsession and fountainhead of suffering. There is a rush to live, to experience, that shudders through the particular animal; but there is no understanding and no in-built purpose beyond the imbecilic repetition of birth, aging, and death. The animal wants life and sensation and the satisfaction of its hunger, and it gets these and loses these monotonously. So revolves the wheel of existence.

Sometimes when we study the animal world we entertain thoughts like these, animal life seeming so circumscribed, pointless, and futile. But we are slower to see our own life in such terms, even though we have the intellectual power to do so. It galls and worries us, of course, even on this gentle morning when a crimson sun dissolves the mist and the bus swings us from one adventure to another. Nature deals with us more liberally—gives us the skill to escape predators and keep ourselves regularly fed and variously entertained—yet still we are born and die in strife. Like these birds we perform marvels in the air of imagination for a little time, amazing one another by swooping from one empty space to another; but the performance soon ends—the props and masks are put away—and we must surrender the energy of our bodies and minds to an unguessable future. We can leave children behind, but that is a thin consolation, for although they may still stand fresh and hopeful when we are spent, can we seriously imagine that their own predicament will be any different? Shall we put off on them the task of figuring out the world, we having given up?

We former children, in the rush of going someplace we cannot this moment remember, smell the wet sweet air and wonder at the white bird rising before us like an omen or a challenge or a symbol of our yet unperfected life. What have we come to? Our parents once stood over our sleep in the late evening, fatigued and sad and full of care, willing us into a future of brightness and safety, and we, unknowing, only sighed and dreamed of wings, and kept on dreaming through the deceitful years. And now, expelled from childhood and loaded with our own duties and regrets, hardly awake even now, looking about with pathetic expectation, we catch this rosy light, this minute drama through the window of a bus. There it is, the lovely, fearful vision of what we are, and behind it, undeniable, the transporting thought of what we might yet be.

We have slept so long, frowning, afflicted, letting ignorance work upon us. Dreamily we marshal forces of mind, we flourish talents, we design and create, all the time foolishly believing that these abilities belong to us, that they are properties and organs of our particular self. Really they are the wings of the crane, just temporary powers bearing us forward and back in obedience to desire until sickness and age abolish the union. History and our own experience at length testify to the baffling truth that the mysteries of existence cannot be solved just by cogitating, by flapping and flying without guidance. Reason can take us far—and indeed we must have it to make progress toward deliverance—but to traverse the darkest canyons of ignorance we need the direct light of Dhamma, which arises from stillness and mindfulness. We have to observe patiently, without bias or fantasy, until the accumulated force of wholesome conditions sparks the flash of insight, the genuine, direct knowing of things just as they exist.

On this rare morning there seems no sense in postponing needful work, so perhaps a brave and forthright way of dealing with the seeming futility of nature is simply to acknowledge it and get on to fresher business. All collections of matter will disintegrate. Imagined egos exist to be superseded, left behind. Thus if we persist in identifying ourselves with impermanent mental states or works or possessions or beauties near or far we must subscribe as well to their blemishes and defects. There is no freedom here, only dismal bondage. We think, we assume, there is an "I" here but, deep beneath the concept, craving goes on bending our faculties to its own dim end, which is just another frothing of sensation. The fictitious, empty "I" eddies along in the stream of desire—no security at all, no strength, no help to anybody. But if we refuse to trust our weight to that foam, if we renounce our claim to the aggregates of body and mind, we can perceive the world in a promising light as a rich field where freedom can grow. If we acknowledge the repetitive, unsatisfactory nature of this *saṃsāra*, this concatenation of births, we can begin to live deliberately, conscious of a higher goal.

So many ages on the great wheel, so much death-and-forgetting, so many promises unkept and foolishness compounded—and the landscape of opportunity slips away. In another moment the bus will carry us past the glowing scene. And yet, arrested here in a splinter of time, feeling the cold metal of the window frame, hearing the rattling engine beneath us, we contemplate this one bird, this flying emblem of destruction and renewal—and trying for once to look on the impermanent without grief and on beauty without greed.

Here is the living Dhamma, summoning us to deliverance, if only we have the breath and the faith to go. We need not give ourselves up to hedonism or despair or irrationality. The Buddha teaches that craving is the source of our cyclic pain, the cause of repeated birth and death. If we can see that pointless round in the crane's flight, if we can glimpse it in the flux of human generations, in the lines in our own faces, should we not turn with a good will to the Buddha's remedy?

At the beginning of the list of factors of the Noble Eightfold Path stands right view—whose presence suggests that there may be such a thing as *wrong* view, to which we hapless dreamers long have been addicted. Without training and without systematic contemplation we see the world, our busy lives, and the morning flight of birds as enduring and reliable and full of self. They are not so. All conditioned things bear the three marks of existence: impermanence, suffering or unsatisfactoriness, and nonself. To perceive these, to have right view, is not to give in to gloom but rather to relieve the strain of upholding a delusion, and to approach the splendor of the unconditioned.

Are we to follow that crane in admiration only to another marsh, to wade and stab at fish and forget the sky?—or another bird whose wings still beat with purpose, climbing above the swamp of custom and dreams? Born with imperfections, with understanding bent and ignorance rampant, still we can hear the Dhamma, still look up to flashing realities and learn the truths they bear. What then shall we make of this human birth?

We have the chance to answer our parents' hopes with more than wealth or position or framed diplomas—to come of age in virtue, to wake to reality, to conquer fear, and to bequeath to our own children, whose sleep we guard, knowledge as well as love. This human life, baffling intersection of good and evil, battleground of thought, affords us a chance. Mortal as the cranes and fishes, we still have minds that can thwart our presumed destiny, shorten our lonely wandering. However uniform or sorrowful our remembered past or unremembered chain of lives, our future and our children's future are not written yet. Turning our thoughts to the good, reading the lessons of nature, listening to the Dhamma, we begin to shape our destiny.

The window of this bus is not the only one that opens to the light. It is the prepared mind that meets with the miraculous, that does not need to wait for symbols. All forms, pleasing and unpleasing, manifest helpful truths, and by detachment and attention we can see them, can come to understand suffering and the end of suffering—the darkness and the light beyond it. Not frightened, not infatuated, we may pass between the wretched and the heavenly without becoming entangled. This is the voyage to ultimate freedom and liberation. The crane will straggle to its end in the weeds, but why should we despair? It rises this morning with white wings on the melting air. We can look and let it alone. Ungrasped, it flies more beautifully.

12. *The Private Version*

🌿 IF WE ARE NEW TO THE STUDY of Buddhism, and are
for the first time becoming acquainted with its analysis of this flawed
world, we might wonder if traditional Buddhism is a little too somber
or too quiescent or passive, and thus perhaps needs some modification
or revision to make it fully appealing to us. The canonical emphasis on
suffering and mental purification, so rare and unsettling for our gener-
ation, prompts various doubts: Shouldn't we be more positive in our
outlook? Shouldn't we emphasize the beauty and delight in the world?
And is there a need to bring in the whole body of the Dhamma when
the practice of meditation together with a few general principles might
suffice for our benefit in busy, dazzling, and demanding society?

Always in the human creature two longings contend: the longing
for pure truth and the longing for individual security. They are seen
to be separate, and we know what choice (sometimes with private
regret) we usually make. But the Buddha teaches that *saṃsāra*, the
round of becoming, seethes with suffering and burns with greed,
hatred, and delusion, within and without, above and below, while
happiness and escape and a *lasting* security are possible by way of the
Noble Eightfold Path. What can we do with such a disturbing teaching? We can follow it in theory and practice toward deliverance, or
we can ignore it, mask it, blend it with our private preferences.

Anxious to believe in a benign, harmonious universe, we might shrink from the deep implications of the Dhamma and try to find security in the practice of meditation simply as a spiritual avocation or an exercise in self-adjustment. But as many meditators have discovered, benefits do not automatically result from the employment of mechanical technique alone. Understanding of the world requires attention, analysis, and clear awareness. Buddhism presents a complete framework for investigation, with morality to lighten and protect the mind, with concentration to assemble its powers, and with wisdom to discern and expel unwholesome qualities.

In all mental training—in all daily life, in fact—the seeker must arouse energy and use it mindfully and skillfully. The systematic setting up of mindfulness (satipaṭṭhāna) results in vipassanā—insight into impermanence, suffering, and nonself. The practice presses toward liberation, the ultimate security, based on this insight—always toward renunciation, not attachment; toward equanimity, not passion; toward purification, not carelessness.

Obviously this is a difficult program. Most people prefer to devote themselves to the satisfactions and rewards of the customary social life, and the Buddha probably never expected otherwise; but he surely meant, at the least, that those of us actively involved in the busy world should not forget the ideal, the pure vision, of the higher way of striving, and should push toward it whenever possible. Yet sometimes, under the weight of habit, we might be inclined to lower our aspirations and even to neglect the ideal in favor of an eager admiration for the world. Perhaps we try to believe that meditation will serve its purpose if it enables us to tolerate our shortcomings, or to appreciate more exquisitely the objects of the senses, or to obtain tranquil feelings. Certainly meditation and the other aspects of the Dhamma smooth out and ease ordinary life here and now, but by quieting mundane desire rather than by gratifying it; and the path rises gradually but steadily into finer atmospheres and worthier thoughts, requiring of the pilgrim faith and perseverance.

A good teacher disrupts his students' vain caprices. We are glad enough to listen, yet probably we would prefer to hear that which would bolster our own half-formed vision of how the world ought to be. Perhaps we want to hear that as long as we keep a meditative and generally amiable frame of mind we can do pretty much as we wish, drifting along casually through life; but the Buddha teaches that our intentional deeds are significant and therefore require attention, that deeds growing out of greed, hatred, and delusion are unwholesome and produce painful results regardless of our wishes or rationalizations. Or we may want to hear that moral precepts are merely admirable, general ideals and not strictly binding on us; but the Buddha regards morality as the indispensable companion to concentration and wisdom, as well as a distinguishing mark of the wise. Or we may want to become comfortably reconciled to our own problematical personalities; but the Buddha teaches that we harbor deep and reprehensible stains which we should clean away. Or we may want to hear that, despite our secret sorrows, the universe we live in is ultimately sublime and perfect; but the Buddha reveals it as a frightful cycle of being-born and dying that offers no permanent security. Thus, with regard to what we might *want*, he is a most contrary and unaccommodating teacher.

Yet the Buddha is always timely and helpful because he speaks directly to abiding human needs, knowing what will actually be of use. In teaching the truth he always stands free of the whims and flutters of fashion. If his powerful focus on suffering is inappropriate for our times or tastes then so is liberation, because there can be no liberation without the prior knowledge that there is bondage, and a spiritual titillation is all we can expect of religion undertaken frivolously, for trivial ends. If we disregard the troubling and provocative teachings of the Buddha and mix the remainder with our private, self-comforting notions, we will come up with a bland something (not a philosophy, not a religion, surely) that requires of us nothing we are not already willing to give and teaches us nothing of value and removes not a jot of our pain.

Accustomed to easy improvising, we might shy away from traditional Buddhist doctrine because the idea of an ancient, fixed formulation suggests intimidating dogma that we will be expected to believe and obey without proof. The classic Dhamma, however, is visible in our own experience, in formal meditation and in daily life. But we can hardly verify something we have not understood in the first place; we can only experience a mass of sensation. Without knowledge of *ends* as well as means, Buddhist philosophy and meditation may become just another dreary search for stimulation.

What we resist so passionately, deep in our minds, is the truth that the very reflex of wanting and grasping by which we have lived is a barb and a torment. While we may disapprove of others' desires, we would like to believe that our own desires are reasonable and legitimate and that life is or could be wonderful, joyful, and full of satisfaction if we could just relax sufficiently, could make some small painless adjustment in perception. Nevertheless an intellectual disquiet troubles us, and religious aspiration erupts from our fear that we are living in a delusive security. We try to be positive in our outlook, but the course of nature is evidently not improved by our commentary. If we tell ourselves, "Yes, this is good," when it is not good, when we are full of grievances, have we accomplished anything? Lacking an understanding of suffering and its cause, we find ourselves doggedly smiling but feeling no smile within.

The Buddha saw that life in the human plane is an uncertain combination of pleasure and pain. He asserted that what there was of enjoyment in the world he had understood, and what there was of misery in the world he had understood, and, furthermore, what there was of *escape* from the world he had also understood. It is wrong to say that Buddhism teaches that everything in the world is entirely miserable and painful. Obviously much gladness, pleasure, grace, and good exist—and more can arise if the conscientious person makes the right efforts. What *can* be said is that everything of a worldly nature is *dukkha*—tenuous, ultimately unsatisfactory, and unreliable—and that in reaching unwisely for the desired or fleeing unwisely from the undesired we continue to flounder and defeat ourselves. The Buddha's path is an even path, not swerving to either extreme of greed or aversion, but leading out of confusion to freedom.

We are invited by the Buddha and the sages of old to take strong Dhamma for our ills, but if we prefer our self-made, imaginary concoctions that is our privilege. If we go on to think them curative, we will be pursuing an easy and familiar course. Certainly in the acquisitive hustle of modern society self-restraint is not popular; renunciation is not popular; moral discipline is not popular. They sound constricting—and indeed they are to base intentions—but they are the limbs and powers of genuine Dhamma and the bringers of contentment. Real peace of mind does not come without effort, and that effort must be guided not by fantasy but by understanding of what really yields lasting benefit.

Sometimes, in the midst of self-doubt and anxiety, we might tend to think that the original Dhamma was suitable for ancient India but that a modernized and adapted version would be better for our own personal circumstances in this sophisticated age. But this is to assume that Dhamma is a historic expression and that modern Dhamma should match modern predilections and accommodate modern wishes. It is reassuring, perhaps, to think that religion might be more or less shaped to our taste, that we can pick up agreeable beliefs here and there and wear them as long as they please us.

But the Buddha teaches Dhamma as a universal description not bound by time or distance, and if we are to seriously investigate it and make use of it we must confront the question, "Is humanity's mortal situation essentially any different now from in the past?" Certainly the people of the Buddha's time had to face old age, sickness, and death as we do, and were no more eager than we to recognize the extent of suffering; but they found refuge and cheer in the Dhamma—so much that they passed on the teaching to their descendants, enabling it to survive through these many centuries. If, as the Buddha declared, craving is the origin of suffering, then its eradication is and will be the solution to the problem, regardless of external conditions. If the noble truths of suffering and the origin of suffering still lie beneath the appearance of things then so must the truth of the cessation of suffering and the truth of the Noble Eightfold Path itself.

This seems plain enough, yet because of the influence of our entrenched habits of thought we might be reluctant to dwell on this grand theme. For easy digestion a private version of Dhamma might seem preferable to us, one that pays perhaps somewhat less attention to the central problem of suffering and more to what we hope are the advantages of appreciating the world without worrying overmuch about our own religious uncertainty and moral responsibility. We know we have weaknesses and failings, but we would much rather treat them as minor matters we can tolerate and forget. Naturally we need some self-respect and hope for the good to come, and certainly we must recognize our present limitations, in the sense that a workman must make do with the materials he has to work with, not despairing over their imperfections, but supinely tolerating our own foolishness and error is tantamount to resolving not to improve ourselves.

Modern society, moreover, enchanted with superficial, material things, effectively encourages a perpetual search for novel experience—a hasty will to grasp, sample, and savor anything within reach, with little concern for danger or real advantage. We ought not, however, to be so reckless, craving being quick enough already to overrun contemplation. Anyway, with our senses avidly functioning, we can hardly help contacting the world, or meeting a multitude of interesting impressions. In the meantime we have chronic sorrows and pains we need to get rid of, and fluttery enthusiasms for one thin inspiration after another only squander energy and delay the necessary confrontation with ignorance, craving, and aversion within our own minds. Are we really discovering, or only dreaming and improvising? As practitioners of the Dhamma we can rely on mindfulness to open the way to knowledge by exposing all ideas, experiences, and emotions to a revealing light, by showing them in their unadorned condition so we can deal with them safely. We need not only to observe bad tendencies, not only to acknowledge their presence, but also to resist them and conquer them, acting with right effort, not merely relaxing into the dim and hazy hope that they will vanish if left alone.

We must admit the fact that there are things wrong with us—defilements, imperfections, hindrances—that no amount of rationalization and self-affirmation will cure, and that, left in place, will continue to pain us and deprive us of peace. When, therefore, we turn to religion for relief from hurt, fear, and confusion, we need more than tremulous hopes for our own betterment. We need a calm, unbiased vision of what is actually happening when we intend and act. We need to hear the ring of bedrock truth—the uplifting Dhamma that is good in the beginning, good in the middle, and good in the end.

When we are doubtful, wondering how to find the energy to observe and expel defilements within us and how far we might venture into the Dhamma as a living faith, it helps especially to entertain the thought of death. The Buddha recommended the contemplation on death (*maraṇānussati*) as bringing "high reward and blessing." He advised meditating monks to reflect at the close of day or in the morning on the many possibilities for sudden death, and then to consider: "Are there still found in me unsubdued evil, unwholesome things that, if I should die today or in this night, would lead me to misfortune?" If such things are found then one should use one's "utmost determination, energy, exertion, perseverance, steadfastness, mindfulness, and clear comprehension in order to subdue these evil and unwholesome things" (*Aṅguttara Nikāya* VIII, 74). Note that we are to subdue them—not tolerate them dreamily or fatalistically. In time all artifices will fall, and we will see whether our gains are real or not. If our practice has been a mere indulging of our favorite illusions the benefit will turn out to be nil. Therefore, as mortal beings we had best be sure we have understood as well as experienced, and acted rightly out of that understanding.

It should be clear from this that the Dhamma is not passive. It is a rousing, gladdening message, challenging us to shake off the grief and fear we have suffered so long. This message invigorates the mind, whereas our private versions of truth tend to lull and stultify. The long-honored, ever-fresh Dhamma needs no revision to move the heart and guide the conduct of a man or a woman today, because it is the abiding essence of goodness and peace, which the Buddha kindly taught for the welfare of living beings. It is independent of time, independent of fashion, not serving the tastes of any age but spelling out in plain terms the nature of the universe and the way to overcome sorrow. Like a current of cool water it pours through our minds, freshening our thought, urging us on to countries yet unexplored.

In the end (and in the beginning too, if we could see it) truth and security are inseparable. When we really wish to perceive truth—the underlying nature of things—we must be prepared to listen and watch in silence, opinions put aside. We must give up our spurious comforts and delusions of being wonderful and exceptional, and instead find out where we really stand and where we have yet to go. Then we might gradually put on the security of wisdom. Though the mind may not yet be pure, still we may know it as it is with equanimity and not be unduly upset. Here is real progress along the path, where the work to be done is always more exacting—and more rewarding—than straying through skies of wishful illusion. Here on the factual earth, now as before, the winds may blow cold but they may also blow clean. So let us shake the dust from our coats and our minds, bear with the weather, and read truth in the original.

13. *An Open View*

🌿 MOST OF US BELIEVE that there is more to see, to perceive, than what we now behold, and that by some refinement of our senses or some revelation of nature itself we might push out our horizons and do away with doubt. If we can comprehend sciences and arts, earn our living with skill, manage household and family, should we not be able, given the chance, to get at least some idea of our own position, speed, and destiny in the cosmos? We are frustrated, it seems, by a haze of distortion billowing before our minds and preventing any open and free view. Out at the rim of sense, things are forever blurring into abstraction, slipping off into the great unaccounted-for. The intellect is balked by this haze, and the heart as well. We want to see because we want to understand. We want to understand because—by instinct if nothing else—we believe understanding to be the key to the heart's release. Yet the world out there remains woefully indistinct, and understanding eludes us, for all the grabs and pounces of our imagination. We consult authorities; we dither over theories; we make pilgrimage to those spots where, we hope, the haze might thin out and truth (whatever *that* is) might shine through. Mostly we retire wearily to our dens to rub our sore eyes and heads and glumly complain that whatever is out there is unreachable. We grow older in the suspicion that life is defeating us.

A helpful fund of wisdom, easy to overlook, may be found nearby, just across the road, really, accessible to anyone who will exert himself. It waits there in any season, in all weathers, but let us now for the sake of example go there while autumn is fast sliding off the precipice of winter. Let us go without special expectation, with senses simply alert, into the park or the meadow or the forest beyond the farm, where beauty was saluted and forgotten weeks ago and we can stroll the leaf-drifted paths in silence under somber branches and think about what has become of the exuberance of summer and fall.

For a few days, when the fall color was at its fullest, people brought out cameras and spent an hour looking for picturesque arrangements, but all that is over and done now, the woods denuded, the earth growing colder, nature withdrawn and empty of fun. But for the thinker, the prober of mysteries, it is a good time, because the dreamy mist of summer has blown away and the eye can dart past the ornaments of things and even, perhaps, through the smoke of confusion to the heart of some fact. Let us see what there is to see.

We have been here before, have we not? It helps to compare present time and past time. The one-time visitor to a spot may harvest an insight or two, but chances improve for those who know a place and can remark its gross or subtle changes through seasons and years. So then, in this bright but chilly afternoon we come not as strangers but as occasional visitors, and the forest stretches before us, the same and not the same. We have hardly stepped from the streets and fields into the trees when the curious impression sweeps over us. The woods have expanded. What in summer was a green, secret vault branching into shady, scented corridors is today a long, hilly stretch of stiff trees and silence. It is no mystery, yet a revelation still. Do we look upon the same country? The reference points are the same—the dips in the path that brought us here, a fractured rock, an ancient beech tree—but the indivisible whole locked in our summer memory now spreads before us as only a remainder. We look, as it were, behind the scenery of a play at the rough boards and worn-out draperies that held up the illusion of a self-sufficient universe. Now that the theater's roof has fallen the stuff of illusion lies revealed on the frigid earth in the keen, dispassionate light. We see with surprise the stumps, stones, gullies, and bumpy ground on which the floating green was founded.

What captured our attention in summer were the scents, the seductive tints, the waving leaves and grasses, the singing nebulas of insects, the spider webs strung glittering through sassafras and maple. We gave little attention then to rock, wood, and primitive dirt—taking the dressed-up scene whole in ignorant delight. But now the sunlight, brilliantly cutting through leafless branches, shows us our error. In summer and resplendent fall we hunted truth but met only the sixfold chaos of ignorance, compounded of sight, sound, smell, taste, touch, and thought. We took what we perceived as the given, the substantial panorama through which to brood our way to enlightenment, and we wondered why it would not yield to our passionate gaze and feed our obscure hunger. We thought that only by a more gluttonous swallowing could we digest truth, not suspecting that we got mostly air, not knowing that even the smallest drops of wisdom must be patiently distilled from reality—that the seeking mind must pierce the deceptive play of forms to the single glove or board or scrap of drapery.

Understanding depends on seeing clearly in the spiritual sense, and seeing clearly depends on removing the obstacles within ourselves. That mist of distortion that seems to roll out there in the distance really rolls in us, filming our eyes, corrupting our thought. It is ignorance, anger, bias, passion, foolish lust for this and that—errors which make us read into the world tremendous themes of tragedy or beauty or harmony. Wrapped in mist, we see according to our wants and fears, not according to nature as it really exists. Sages, we are told, dwell contentedly with senses controlled, unconquered by sense desires—but we, who nod at this intelligence, make haste to be conquered, to surrender to sensory influx, to soak ourselves in all kinds of experience in hopes of arousing agreeable feelings.

What is this alluring, grasped-at life after all? Just *nāma* and *rūpa*—mental and material factors perpetually arising and vanishing. We perceive the world through the operation of the six sense bases of eye, ear, nose, tongue, body, and mind. Each internal sense base has its corresponding object or external sense base: the eye and visible forms; the ear and sounds; the nose and odors; the tongue and flavors; the body and tangible objects; the mind and mental objects. When forms contact the eye, visual consciousness arises; when sounds contact the ear, auditory consciousness arises. Likewise, when appropriate objects engage the other sense bases there arise smell consciousness, taste consciousness, touch consciousness, and mental consciousness. Analyzed in this way, there are six types of consciousness—not the comprehensive single one we imagine as a self or identity—and each type occurs through the operation of a particular sense faculty. Our experience—our perceiving and knowing—is thus not monolithic but various, dependent, conditioned, dynamic, flashing up in a continuous stream of events.

How then might we confront this stream without being overwhelmed with confusion? The Buddha advised one questioner to train himself in this way: "In the seen there will be merely what is seen; in the heard there will be merely what is heard; in the sensed there will be merely what is sensed; in the cognized there will be merely what is cognized" (*Udāna* 1.10). This means that all sensory impressions on eye, ear, nose, tongue, body, and mind should be noted factually as what they are in themselves, as distinct phenomena, not warped by liking or disliking, not embroidered with vain imaginings. The careful thinker, when considering objects, tries to understand the compounded, changing nature of phenomenal reality, knowing that *all* elements are empty of self.

When the season changes and we are freed from leafy distraction we can make out the prosaic wood and earth that support the forest—the rigging for the green illusion. Indeed, if we looked closely enough into those bare trees and shrubs we would find more sham, more artifice, more compounding. We must try not to be thrown off by the marvels of appearance but to investigate deeper reality, not just with intellect—though intellect has its place—but with the intuitive tool of mindfulness, which reaches past bumbling cogitation and theorizing and deals with events directly. In the seen there will be just what is seen, in the heard, just what is heard. This is how we can train the mind, how we can make possible the arising of insight.

There are lessons to be read in the destitution of the forest, in the fragility of all these branches, in the sodden leaves underfoot, in the cold, massive earth. But such lessons of impermanence and emptiness are only signposts on the path. They are not the goal. Ultimate truth is experienced and understood directly, not assembled by logic, not composed by imagination. With the exercise of reason the contemplative person strengthens his mind for intuitive discovery, when insight will bloom. The world "out there" is not remote and inaccessible but right here in this "fathom-long body with its perceptions and thoughts," and this world is ultimately understood and transcended not by theoretical sophistication, not by whipped-up trances, but by steady, calm attention to the messengers of sense. We cannot arrange to perceive only what is delightful, but we can discipline our senses for the true comprehension of whatever appears. With a mind put to work not on fantasies but facts we can find out the shape of the scene around us and realize the steps we must yet take for our safety and freedom.

The air of this transparent day, moved by influences beyond itself, begins to pour across the sunny hills and sway the topmost branches of the woods. We hear a sighing in the twigs and a groaning of the big limbs; woody vines swing stiffly; a crow calls raggedly; a squirrel jumps from oak to beech; and we sigh and stir. Change breaks up all static dreams. What sort of peace is it that depends on flukes of good fortune? Shall we not try to earn a firmer peace? Let the elements dance through our senses as they will; let us feel what we feel but nonetheless try to stay detached from all that. The world reels by in a tempest, but must we run after it? Might we not keep patient in the face of the six wild messengers? A burning stick twirled in the night produces the illusion of fiery script, but the watchful mind suffers no attachment to illusion, seeing the script, the red coal, the twirling stick, and the boundless tumult of nature around them all.

14. *Four Elements*

🍃 O<small>N THIS SUMMER AFTERNOON</small> in the city we have hurried on business through corridors and offices, down shaded pavements and across glaring plazas and avenues, with our thoughts scrambling ahead of our feet toward the next appointment or duty. Harried and intent, we lean forward in our deliberate march, sorting our plans as we make our way deftly through crowds. Now we pause for a street light, now we step out and go on, seeking the shortest route. A city park lies in our way, and we will cross it, settling on the way, if we can, a few details of what we need to do at our next stop.

But the park is wide and the rhythm of walking has time to soften our impetuousness, and we find, looking up with surprise, that today the hot wind romps around us and the sun flashes in our eyes with immediate and refreshing vigor. Here, we reflect, is the world—vivid, concrete, bustling with shapes and forces, perceptible, tactile, material. And here too is this breathing human body, another moving shape amid shapes, cognizable through our senses, and real if we can call anything real among all these motes and masses. The park is busy this afternoon with office workers leisurely returning from lunch breaks, and young people playing ball or jogging on dusty pathways, and children running and shrieking through playgrounds or dashing about tugging on the strings of kites. The bordering streets clatter with traffic, while across the sky drift big bulbous clouds, stately, various, and ever-changing.

We feel ourselves expand a little in the bluff physicality of the summer afternoon, pleased by the coarseness of life in the open sunlight. Shall we recover now some lost balance? Where were we in the morning before our attention ran away? Were we not meaning to be more mindful, to contemplate phenomena in the present moment as they swelled and popped like bubbles? But even as we stride and breathe more easily now, trying to get back down from fantasy to the earth again, the intensity of the surrounding scene raises a question. Have we ever really understood this realm of matter, or have we, whenever we peered and scratched at it, used it simply as a gateway into intangible realms of feeling and concept—leaping at once from a simple impression to an ornate mental construction? Let us slow down a little more here; let us not be content with surfaces. The wind-ruffled trees, the plump clouds, the grass whisking against the shoe, and the feet (apparently ours) that carry our weight—what *are* they in fact, and how should we regard them?

According to Buddhism, material form (*rūpa*) is one of the five aggregates of existence, the others being feeling, perception, mental formations, and consciousness. There is the *rūpa* that constitutes our own bodies, and there is the *rūpa* that constitutes external objects. None of this material form, however, within or without, can rightly be regarded as being a self or belonging to a self, nor even as any unquestionable foundation of reality, because it is all impermanent, unstable, subject to dissolution. Moreover, it is all conditionally arisen; it does not stand on its own but depends on various supporting factors.

The plain, seemingly factual matter we see and touch is actually composed of four basic material elements (*mahā-bhūta*): the earth element, the water element, the fire element, and the air element. The names do not refer to literal ingredients but rather *characteristics* that are present to various degrees in physical objects, that in fact determine the appearance of those objects to our senses. The earth element is the characteristic of solidity, of hardness or softness. The water element is the characteristic of fluidity or cohesion. The fire element is the characteristic of heat and cold, of temperature. The air element is the characteristic of motion. These elements, in varying proportions, constitute the perceived physical universe in all its immensity and complexity. They are, it should be understood, mere characteristics or qualities, not singly or all together any kind of durable essence or identity.

Within one's own body the earth element manifests itself most notably in the more solid parts, such as hair, nails, teeth, and bones. Other liquid parts, such as tears, sweat, and blood, exemplify the water element. The air element is present in the form of gases, as in the air surging in and out of the lungs. The fire element is present in the heating processes of the body, as in the digestion of food. These same characteristics of solidity, fluidity, heat, and motion permeate, compose, and define all material form outside the body as well. From them the variegated objects of the world get their distinctive appearance as grass, clouds, kites, living bodies, scuffed-up dust, and concrete cities.

There is no difference between the primary elements within the body and those outside it: the earth element is everywhere simply the earth element; water is water; fire is fire; air is air. That is to say, the quality of solidity is intrinsically the same within and without, as are fluidity, heat, and motion. Beneath the astonishing multiplicity and variety of the physical universe there is to be found just the sameness, the impersonality of these elements. All of them, according to the Buddha, should be seen for what they are and regarded in this way: "This is not mine, this is not what I am, this is not my self" (*Majjhima Nikāya* 28). If one in fact regards the physical elements and the objects built out of them in this way one will lose one's compulsive appetite for them and will be moved to turn away from them, to cease running after them in their various guises; and this is exactly the point of Buddhist analysis and contemplation of material form. From craving there arise the numberless kinds of suffering, and this craving is traceable to and supported by a persistent ignorance about the nature of reality. When, therefore, the investigator perceives and considers the component parts of the objects of his senses, down even to these bare elements or qualities, he begins to erode the ignorance that has so long kept up suffering. With a growing knowledge of what really composes and holds together attractive and repulsive forms, he becomes less susceptible to craving, and as craving fades so does suffering.

But why is it, we might wonder, that craving for material things—these blends of earth, water, fire, and air that seem so much more trustworthy than the shadowy stuff of the mind—should necessarily lead to suffering? On such a brave summer day as this, as we admire the colorful kites that shake and soar, we feel, for the moment, a sense of comfort and—let us admit—a gush of intense *liking* for many agreeable objects in our view. The world jumps at us with its sounds and scents and colors, and we can hardly keep from welcoming them. To be *obsessed* with material things is surely bad, but might we not frankly call some of them good and desirable and get what we can out of them? Does being compounded of impersonal elements necessarily detract from their worth?

Let us look further, then, into Buddhist doctrine to find our way, if we can, both to understanding and to peaceful dwelling in the world. Craving is, first of all, a state of incompleteness and tension and imbalance. If the interval between the onset of craving and its satisfaction is long enough we can clearly recognize it as frustration—a manifestly painful condition. As the Buddha points out, not getting what we want is a kind of suffering. But even if craving quickly attains its goal the gratification is often a paltry, disintegrating thing, a shabby compensation for the itch and the effort involved. Our minds mislead us; we have imagined richer reward than was actually forthcoming; so disappointment descends—another kind of suffering. Feeling disappointed, we allow craving to gather itself again and launch out in another direction, and the dismal process continues.

And why should our minds mislead us? Simply because we have not perceived rightly to begin with; we have not understood things as they really exist; we have not comprehended the fundamental emptiness of the objects that attract us or repel us. We skip over the task of systematic observation and inquiry, giving no thought to the elements or factors beneath appearance. Agitated by heedless desire, assuming stability in what is unstable, and lacking knowledge of the compounded nature of things, we habitually wander into error.

These appealing forms, these concrete objects of bulk and volume that seem to offer what is most real and reliable, that strike our senses so insistently, do not yield and cannot yield what we most hope for—

a complete and *undying* gratification. The Buddha was perfectly aware that the world abounds in enjoyable things, but he saw their fatal imperfection—their impermanence. When confused and uninformed beings passionately pursue what is temporary, provisional, and sure to change, misery is to be expected. When craving arises, suffering will follow.

Material forms, for all their perceived solidity and immediacy, are conditionally arisen and, whether they change slow or fast, subject to dissolution. We might label as good or valuable some of the colorful and appealing forms surrounding us on this fine day, but we ought to realize that they certainly will not *remain* so, and this fact indeed should be counted against their presumed intrinsic worth. It is not that beautiful things are necessarily unreal, only that their reality, their actual nature, is variable, conditioned, fleeting, and incapable of satisfying our desires for permanent pleasure.

Beautiful objects and pleasant experiences are part of our world and not bad in themselves. The person who works hard, who fulfills his or her duties, and who behaves virtuously will in time, in this world or another, receive various sorts of good fortune, like wealth and health and comfort, and these are, relatively speaking, advantageous and gratifying things. Yet none of these—neither material possessions nor pleasant sensory experiences nor even the blessing of long life—ought to be confused with the *ultimate* good.

A physical object—a chair or a leaf or a clod of earth—is a compound of impersonal, empty qualities, and this fact is important to us because, whether the object is beautiful, valuable, delightful, or useful to us, knowing its actual, transitory nature can prevent us from craving it ignorantly, grasping it foolishly, and suffering as a consequence. Mindful contemplation of material form, as well as of the four mental aggregates, corrects our tendency to latch on to things greedily and gives a sense of moderation and balance that will be invaluable for the attainment of enlightenment.

One variety of material form that we particularly need to contemplate is this human body itself. It is the object with which we are most deeply and immediately concerned—though probably more by instinct than by detailed observation, and more when pain erupts than when comfort prevails. In the lack of reflection or the lack of good instruction to the contrary, we habitually consider the body as "me" or "my body," and, assuming we can keep it healthy, as a source of pride, satisfaction, and self-confidence; or else, in the unhappy case of illness or injury, as a source of pain, shame, and anxiety. Among all changing, disintegrating, fluctuating shapes it is the one we most urgently intend to preserve, to embellish, and to serve.

Because the human body is so marvelous in its complexity and its abilities, it may be a surprise to learn that Buddhism, far from admiring and praising this preeminent object, regards it with notable coolness, with wary detachment, as an assemblage of parts of no inherent charm. The body, in the Buddhist view, is neither to be adored nor tormented; it is to be investigated with the same precision and detachment as the mental factors of the human personality. That the body is central to our happiness and our suffering we can readily understand, but we learn from the Pali texts that the body may also be a prime means to enlightenment:

> One thing, O monks, if developed and frequently practiced, leads to a deep stirring of the mind; to great benefit, to great security from toil; to mindfulness and clear comprehension; to the attainment of vision and knowledge; to a happy abiding in this very life; to the realization of the fruit of knowledge and deliverance. What is that one thing? It is the mindful contemplation of the body.
>
> (Aṅguttara Nikāya I, 21)

The Buddha recommends various kinds of contemplation of the body, such as mindfulness of breathing, contemplation of the postures or positions that the body can assume, and careful awareness of the physical processes involved in moving about, eating, and carrying out all the activities of daily life. Moreover, the Buddha recommends the contemplation of the body's impure parts—such as skin, bones, sinews, blood, and many other organs—in the way that one might impersonally investigate a sack full of different kinds of grain. With this objective attitude one may analyze the body in terms of its basic elements—the solidity, fluidity, heat, and motion that underlie its conventional appearance. Furthermore, the meditator may consider the body as if it were dead and thrown away and passing through the natural stages of decomposition down to mere bones and dust— constantly reflecting in this way: "This body of mine also has this nature, has this destiny, and cannot escape it." Thus he cools down his painful fever of attachment, chastens vanity, and readies himself to live peacefully with reality.

In all these contemplations the aim of the meditator is to overcome his innate attachment to the body and understand it clearly and unsentimentally in its conditionally arisen and perishable nature. Of such a person the Buddha says:

> *He abides contemplating the body as a body in this way either in himself, or externally, or in himself and externally. Or else he contemplates in the body either its factors of origination, or its factors of fall, or its factors of origination and fall. Or else mindfulness that "There is a body" is established in him to the extent of bare knowledge and remembrance of it while he abides independent, not clinging to anything in the world. That is how a monk abides contemplating the body as a body.*
>
> (Dīgha Nikāya 22; Majjhima Nikāya 10)

Such exercises can free the meditator from bondage, clinging, worry, and fear regarding the body, and make way for equanimity based on mature understanding. The body is ultimately just *rūpa* or matter, just neutral, material elements in dynamic and temporary association, but on account of ignorance it becomes a focus of ferocious craving, fascination, lust, fear, obsession, and vanity. Mindful contemplation of the body's usually ignored unattractive aspects serves to pull the over-reaching mind back to a healthy balance.

But on such a splendid afternoon as this, entertained by fresh breezes, surrounded by vigorous, vibrant people running, exercising, playing ball in a scene of sunny recreation, we might feel quite disinclined to reflect on the disagreeable characteristics of the human body. We are perhaps privately even a little embarrassed that we feel *any* revulsion toward the body, for is it not the predominant opinion of our society that the body is (or at least *should* be) beautiful, admirable, entrancing, magnificent, glorious? Still, perhaps more than a glance across these happy acres of parkland is needed; perhaps what is *absent* from the scene has significance. The realities of humanity do not correspond with its fantasies and ideals; if we look closer at these laughing faces and muscular forms bobbing past us, we notice that these are mostly *young* people, certainly well fed and obviously free from debilitating illness. Where are the aged, the exhausted, the sick, the incapacitated? If we are going to hang on to our dear belief in the loveliness of the body can we exclude them from our thought? If a few hale people are skipping freely over the grass how many others lie groaning in hospital beds, enduring pain?

There are some facts we simply cannot get around. For one thing, the body, no matter how strong and splendid, ages. It does not long retain those characteristics we so admire, but takes on the unwelcome characteristics of age. Furthermore, the body sickens. It shakes and shudders and malfunctions; it gives rise to discomfort, misery, pain. Furthermore, the body dies. Eventually it breaks down entirely and ceases to function. All the qualities we admire in the body are impermanent.

Even if we confine our attention to bodies still vigorous, not yet old or seriously ill, we find support for the Buddhist view. Even a body conventionally considered athletic or beautiful or attractive is decidedly impure, and is kept from appearing so and causing general disgust only by ceaseless effort and ingenuity. Consider the labors that must be performed just to make the body functional and presentable each day—the feeding and chewing and swallowing, the scrubbing of teeth, the washing of skin and hair. Left to itself, even for a short while, the body becomes filthy and begins to stink. This is not an aberration; it is perfectly normal and also, lamentably, disgusting. Such is the nature of the body, a nature we so hastily and automatically disguise that we can, for a time, actually forget there is any impurity present at all. But only for a time. Despite our unwillingness to pay attention, change, age, illness, or uncleanliness eventually breaks into our awareness; desire is driven away from one material form and hurries to fasten upon another whose surfaces can meet, for the moment, its fickle and unpredictable requirements. All surfaces and all interiors, however, give way to the assaults of time and illness, and even in radiant youth reveal undeniably repulsive aspects.

Buddhist contemplations of the body are sensible means by which the determined meditator can come to know coarse reality and learn to live intelligently and without unnecessary perturbation. Bodies, we must see, are after all not supernatural wonders but only imperfect, held-together material, *rūpa*, heaps of impure parts not attractive in themselves. Need we upset ourselves so much over them?

Because the body is ever liable to injury, decay, and disease, we cannot trust it too far. It supports us; but in another sense we support it—enduring its indispositions and failures, rushing to attend to its requirements, feverishly anticipating annoyances—and the load may become frightful in times of serious travail if we remain sunk in the conviction that the afflicted body actually *belongs* to us, is inseparable from our self. This is a dangerous form of bondage that the Buddha warns us against, advising us to regard the body as a source of peril and trouble.

> *Now, Aggivesana, this body that has material form consists of the four great elements; it is procreated by a mother and father and built up out of rice and bread; it is subject to impermanence, to anointing and rubbing, to dissolution and disintegration. It must be regarded as impermanent, as suffering, as a boil, as a dart, as a calamity, as an affliction, as alien, as disintegrating, as void, as not self. When he [the wise man] regards it so, he abandons his desire and affection for it and his habit of treating it as the necessary basis for all his inferences.*
> (Majjhima Nikāya 74)

If we regard our own bodies in such ways, with great circumspection and wariness about their potential to cause pain, we will not be drawn into delusion but will experience the independence of thought necessary for overcoming suffering and attaining enlightenment.

But how, we might wonder, are we to treat the body and the whole physical side of life without undue attachment? Here we should remember the great principle of moderation and nonextremism taught by the Buddha in his first discourse:

> *There is devotion to pursuit of pleasure in sensual desires, which is low,*
> *coarse, vulgar, ignoble, and harmful; and there is devotion to self-*
> *mortification, which is painful, ignoble, and harmful. The middle way*
> *discovered by the Tathāgata avoids both these extremes; it gives vision,*
> *gives knowledge, and leads to peace, to direct knowledge, to enlightenment,*
> *to Nibbāna. And what is that middle way? It is this Noble Eightfold*
> *Path; that is to say: right view, right intention, right speech, right action,*
> *right livelihood, right effort, right mindfulness, right concentration.*
>
> (Vinaya Mahāvagga 1:6; Saṃyutta Nikāya 56:11)

Heedlessly indulging in luxury is a harmful extreme, and so also is tormenting or mistreating the body in a mistaken effort at spiritual purification. The body should be treated as a useful vehicle, taken care of, kept clean, nourished moderately, allowed adequate rest, and tended to in illness. It does not require fond attachment, only practical maintenance and repair. We can get a general idea of what the middle way means in this regard by considering the four basic material supports of the Buddhist monk: robes, alms food, shelter, and medicine. In using any of these the well-practicing monk is supposed to reflect properly on their purposes. That is, he uses his robes just to guard himself from cold and heat and biting, stinging creatures, and to cover himself modestly. He takes food not out of greed for pleasure or desire to make his body attractive, but just to allay hunger and to keep the body healthy and comfortable so that he may follow a worthy path of life. He makes use of lodging or shelter for the sake of seclusion and to avoid cold and heat and biting, stinging creatures and the afflictions of weather. He takes medicine to dispel and keep away the painful sensations of illness and to stay in the best health possible.

These are specifically monastic guidelines, but the principles behind them also apply to lay people. The human body has certain basic needs for health, and these ought to be attended to judiciously, simply, in a practical spirit, so that life may be carried on with a minimum of physical suffering, in reasonable comfort, without veering to the dangerous extremes of luxury or self-torment. The Buddha says that before he left the household life he enjoyed great luxury, but eventually he found this unsatisfactory and unsuited to one who was profoundly troubled by the question of suffering; so he gave up such indulgence and left home. Later, as a young ascetic, he strenuously practiced various forms of self-torment, but ultimately he found them useless and profitless. After he reached full enlightenment—after he achieved perfect balance—he practiced and taught a simple, healthy, and energetic style of life.

Material form, of whatever variety, within or outside of the body, is nothing permanent or trustworthy, but only the conditionally arisen, restless combination of solidity, fluidity, heat, and motion. Through intellectual analysis and direct contemplation we can find no self or ego in it, no unchangeable grains of reality, no ultimate gravel or grit. Matter, it seems, is as mysterious and tenuous as mind, and as helpless to furnish satisfaction for craving. We might run to the material shows of the world for comfort or reassurance, but impermanence, suffering, and nonself characterize the material as well as the mental side of existence. Suppose, for example, that we command this material thing, this body that we call "mine," never to get sick or never to grow old and frail. What will happen? Suppose we stipulate that flowers shall not fade in our house nor food grow stale. What will happen? So poor is our power, so absurd our ownership.

As we walk or stand or turn about, shading our eyes on this brilliant afternoon, remembering the teaching of the Buddha, we might begin to wish for a peace beyond all grasping, beyond the ghostly pretense of the elements. Let us do our day's work; let us feel the refreshing breeze but not detain it—it is not ours, but only the air element, impersonal and restless. The ground, yielding or hard, and the waters that ripple in fountains are only manifestations of these continuous processes of nature. If we claim any of these as *ours* we will suffer with their inevitable change; if we let them go on their way we will not suffer on their account.

When we attach ourselves to material forms, thinking to find lasting happiness in the crude certainty of what can be touched, eaten, drunk, worn, etc., we fool ourselves and become dismayed spectators at processes that run away from us, out of control. When the necessary physical organs are functioning together, supporting one another, we say there is a "body" present, but our naming does not confer on it any effective identity or power to withstand change; it is still a complex of parts that, having been put together through past *kamma* working through the patterns of chemistry and biology, must necessarily break down and become scattered again in time. Our greed and aversion regarding the body are mental phenomena which arise based on a mistaken view of the body, an ignoring of its compounded and transient nature. Our food and drink as well, our clothes and furniture and houses and all material things we look to for our health and comfort should be viewed correctly not as the appurtenances of an ego but only as empty and perishable forms which should not be allowed to drive us from our right course.

And what *is* our right course? Kites dance across the sky this afternoon like gleeful signs, but they dance according to the wind and the limiting string. The strolling crowds unravel in all directions, moved by a thousand desires. We have our own intentions, our business, our errands of the moment on which our feet are carrying us, but beyond all errands do we have a goal that is worthy to pursue? Shall we be always distracted by the flickering spectacle of earth, water, air, and fire and wander beguiled through an endless gallery of forms? Or shall we, by patient mindfulness and considered effort, make our contemplative course more sure and straight toward the end of all suffering and the highest emancipation?

Now the grass gives out and we have concrete underfoot again. The metal and glass of automobiles throw off brilliance; buildings swing by in the varying din, in the bustling air. Still our journey continues. A body is walking, but it is not ours. A breath comes and goes, ownerless. Clouds cruise majestically above. Eye, ear, nose, tongue, body, and mind register impressions. Not in the exploitation of any of these is our peace to be found, but rather in the calm understanding of them and the letting go of them. Shall we always be pulled along by rollicking kites on strings? All scenes pass; all forms dissolve. The diligent seeker after the good, moral in his actions, kindly disposed toward living beings, contemplates what comes and goes until, emptied of delusion, enriched with vision, he releases all, and knows himself released.

15. The Question of Progress

🍃 THOSE WHO UNDERTAKE long or difficult journeys do not usually do it for the sake of the scenery alone. They have a destination in mind, the thought of which inspires them in the first place and keeps them going through all kinds of country. On journeys of the religious sort, as well as the purely geographical, travelers want to learn that they are making progress toward the goal that they have set for themselves or that appears simply necessary to them. Buddhists, like everyone else, want to get somewhere and to finish what they have begun; and if they are determined, they find that undertaking the path of Dhamma confers benefits that are directly and presently visible. Thus it is possible to obtain some idea of progress, although this progress may, paradoxically, come as heightened understanding of what is *yet* to be done.

We might not concern ourselves so much with progress if the emphasis of the Dhamma were on faith more than on action. We then might merely await, as a reward for our faith or constancy, some approaching deliverance. But when we have come to see the universe as vastly uncertain, vastly and challengingly free, and when the idea sinks into us that *we* are ultimately responsible for our own happiness or unhappiness in past, present, and future, then we feel more and more the need to shake off the fear or paralysis that now grips us and to make our way to safer ground. That gentle smile on the visage of the Buddha that history and art record both calms us and draws us forward. Somewhere ahead, beyond the forbidding obstacles of the day, lie serenity and sweetness. We want to see the mileposts passing, to breathe cleaner air, and to be assured that our exertions count for something.

This is not to say that faith is unimportant. Faith, in Buddhism, has more the nature of confidence than of passive belief, and it underlies the striving of the disciple who, having seen that the Buddha's advice has proven good so far, is willing to trust him further, testing and confirming with warmer devotion. Sometimes too much is made of the analytical, logical aspect of the Dhamma, as if faith were an embarrassing relic that should be quickly discarded. Yet intellectual study by itself does not secure freedom, sterile technique falls short, and baseless theorizing only misleads. The Dhamma, rightly practiced, engages both the sympathies and the intellect; it unites the fragments of human sensibility into a healthy whole and makes possible a balanced progress toward happiness and security.

In outline form, it might go like this. Someone hears the teaching of the Buddha—the profound revelation of the cause and the cure of suffering. He ponders the meaning of the Dhamma and, looking around at the world, begins to see aspects of those truths everywhere reflected back at him. Curious, wondering, watching, he notices that things, events, and people seem to conform to the laws of Dhamma, and he feels the first surge of elation and hope that this indeed might be the way for him. He begins to act on the first principles of giving, morality, and concentration of mind, and soon notices a lightness in his spirits and a sense of expanded clarity and self-control. Faith awakes in him and grows brighter, side by side with his investigating consciousness. Inspired and cheered, he realizes there is more to be done in the way of practice and more to be gained in the way of freedom. Putting forth effort, he magnifies his blessings, and in recognizing those blessings he understands he is making progress.

Throughout the Pali texts there are many references to stages of practice and levels of achievement, such as seven stages of purification, four supermundane paths and four fruitions, four meditative absorptions, and four immaterial spheres. Progress is also noted in reverse fashion in the abandonment of harmful conditions. These categories and formulations are worth studying in the texts, as they not only describe from various standpoints the journey to liberation but impress on the student's mind the dynamic and cumulative nature of the Dhamma so that there can be no mistaking both the existence of higher and higher levels of attainment and the advantages of reaching them. A sound theoretical knowledge will also help steer one away from dead ends in meditation and unjustified self-criticism or self-congratulation. If one knows that a certain level of achievement is characterized by specific virtues and abilities, then one can more accurately gauge the state of one's practice. Lacking such knowledge, new practitioners might think they are getting nowhere or, with more optimism than judgment, might erroneously suppose themselves very advanced.

While it is true that only the practical training of the mind can cause true insight to arise, we may be sure that the Buddha did not speak so many discourses on Dhamma for nothing. He wanted his disciples to make progress, and to that end he taught them precise details about the nature of the aggregates of existence, the functioning of the senses, the deeds to be done and those not to be done, the arising and ceasing of defilements, and more. People differ in their capacity to absorb doctrine, and it is noteworthy that the Buddha taught with a shrewd awareness of his hearers' situations, capabilities, and personal biases, giving to some only the simplest moral injunctions and encouragement to practice generosity, and to others detailed explanations of the processes of nature. The Buddha overburdened nobody, but taxed his followers to the limits of their ability—and exhorted them to expand those limits.

Thus when we attempt to equal the achievements of the disciples of old we ought to see to it that we are as well prepared as they, not necessarily by accumulating great scholarly knowledge (for indeed they varied among themselves in this dimension), but by remembering and pondering available lessons as well as we can. We need not become scholars, but we should at least try to make clear in our own minds the fundamental points of the Buddha's doctrine, so that we can see where and how to employ our energy. Then, as curiosity or need moves us, we may investigate more deeply in the Dhamma. Simply, for useful work we must gather solid information. To build a good house we must have proper tools. To make a safe journey we need a map.

Suppose someone says, "I've read several books and I've been practicing meditation for a good while now and I feel reverence toward the Buddha, the Dhamma, and the Sangha, but I don't feel like I'm making any progress. My mind is still full of turmoil!" As such problems are extremely common among serious practitioners, it would be useful to examine the idea of progress more closely. Upon being introduced to the Dhamma, students might in their enthusiasm hurry past deep, fundamental teachings to get to what they think are the good parts—descriptions of exalted states of mind, psychic powers, the varieties of sainthood, and *Nibbāna*. These descriptions are valuable because they whet the spiritual appetite and stimulate action, but their very attractiveness may cause impatient students to forget the long road to perfection and to wonder why they cannot leap right into it.

Practice of the Dhamma does indeed clarify vision and ease the mind, but often in subtle degrees. In fact, to *know* at a given moment that one has a confused or impatient state of mind is itself an indication of progress. The untutored neophyte, eager to dive into glorious experiences, might have no such awareness and might reject the idea that his mind is not functioning perfectly already. He might be impatient and only hazily conscious of some impediment to the splendor he thinks should be his. But a little intelligent practice reveals that the answers to important questions, and the questions themselves, are deeper and more involved than they seemed at first.

We might think of progress in the Dhamma as a journey out of the wasteland of ignorance into the fruitful fields of knowledge. From false ideas of our own nature and our place in the universe we proceed to clearer and clearer assessments based on impartial observation. In other words, we make progress by learning what we are and where we stand, regardless of whether that is presently agreeable or disagreeable. It is useless to imagine ourselves vaulting over the last barrier to enlightenment when we are presently strolling along an easy road that has scarcely yet begun to rise into the mountains; and it is also useless to mope and delay, supposing we can never leave behind our stiff and stifling habits and go where we ought to go.

In a morning's walk or an evening's meditation we may be conscious of mental commotion, confusion, and anxiety. Instead of moaning, "Oh, I'm not getting anywhere!" we would do better to reflect: "These mental states are arising and passing away. This is the way the mind is now." Our first object ought to be not to control the mind in all its operations, but to know the mind. If we can simply note pleasurable or painful or neutral phenomena as they occur without instantly interpreting them, commenting on them, or embracing them as "mine," we are moving in the right direction. Many of our problems come from not knowing, not seeing things directly and accurately, and consequently behaving foolishly. To get along expeditiously we must pay attention to mind and body at the present moment, in their present condition. Nobody can outrun his own feet.

But if the path is as true and fine as it is supposed to be, why is it that we have such a hard time getting our feet out of the mud? Why can't we move faster? No doubt we would waste no time in making our way to liberation were it not for certain troublesome factors called the five hindrances (*nīvaraṇa*). The first of these is sensuous desire, the recurrent fascination with the objects of the senses, which tugs the mind away from its work and beguiles it with sight, sound, smell, taste, touch, and imagination. The second hindrance is ill will, which means all degrees of animosity toward others. The third is lethargy and drowsiness. The fourth is agitation and worry. The fifth is skeptical doubt—not the investigative reserve of the careful thinker but rather compulsive disbelief and timidity regarding the Dhamma.

These five pestiferous agents act to weaken us and deter us from practicing. So normal, so natural, so intrinsically part of *us* do they seem that we often have difficulty in recognizing them as impersonal and harmful mental irritants; and under their influence we think too literally, "*I* want, *I* dislike, *I* am tired, *I* am agitated, *I* am doubtful." Beneath the ordinary use of language lurks a tenacious delusion of self that keeps us from seeing what is really going on. Sensuous desire entices us here and there with gaudy trifles so that we forget our duty. Ill will roils up the heart so that concentration falls apart. Lethargy and drowsiness drain away our vigor and stupefy us with illusions of weakness and fatigue, with a droning suggestion that we do not have the strength for practice. Agitation and worry attack us from another extreme, setting us to fantasizing, scheming, fretting, like mice gnawing on a board—in quite a difficult condition for carrying out impartial observation. Skeptical doubt infiltrates the mind in the guise of judgment and whispers, "Maybe the Dhamma is wrong. What if this is all a waste of time? This is too hard for me. Maybe I should give up." And on and on endlessly with this tune.

Fortunately, the five hindrances are not invincible. They slow progress but do not make it impossible. Therefore, when we are concerned about our seeming inability to move ahead we should remember to note the hindrances, as they appear, just as impermanent tendencies that, like all phenomena, rise and fall according to conditions. Confront them—they retreat. Push at them—they give way. These legions of deleterious thoughts and moods that assail us draw their power from our ignorance of their real nature. Enchanted since birth, we fear shadows and mirages, but the experience of Dhamma, with its radical revelation of fundamentals, breaks enchantment and discloses the freedom and responsibility that have always been ours.

How to reform this recalcitrant mind is a question best answered by the journey along the path of discovery itself. We are often naively intent on making the mind behave exactly the way we would like it to behave—an impossible undertaking, as we find out to our disappointment. Then we wrongly conclude we have not made or cannot make progress. But when we stop predicting what we should encounter and simply study what arises and how it arises, then we have made the first strides toward understanding and training the mind. It should be no disgrace to learn that we have frailties, that we cannot hold concentration for more than a few consecutive seconds, that our attention is carried off by absurd whims. This very looking and this calm awareness hasten the birth of liberating insight.

When the mind is burdened with defilement—troubled with anger, greed, resentment, pride, and other unwholesome qualities—we should try to know it as it is, without reacting automatically. When a thought, a volition, a memory, or a desire appears we may mark the place, mark the moment with a light, comprehending glance. This is how equanimity can come to be—by putting aside the temptation to get tangled up in mental circuses and instead acknowledging with minute awareness the arising and dissolution of jostling phenomena. When we watch, sensitive to subtle influences, we see that each instance of aversion or craving erupts from prior conditions, lasts a while, and fades away, to be followed by more little twinges. Why should we vex ourselves about this or that droplet in the waterfall of time? The job of the meditator is not to decorate the mind with cosmetic imagination but to know, by purposeful attention, how conditioned things, good or bad, succeed one another right in this very moment.

We find ourselves stuck and confused not from lack of ready truths to see but from spiritual vision still hampered by spiritual ills. Complete enlightenment, or arahantship, depends on the destruction of sense desire, desire for eternal existence, wrong views, and ignorance; and such destruction is brought about by stripping off delusion, waving away mist, chasing out laziness, until we confront nature just as it is. Indeed, we must travel, we must make the miles go by; but the astute traveler on this path does not act like a tourist, freighting himself with souvenirs and bric-a-brac, but rather becomes less acquisitive—abandoning oppressive and demoralizing entertainments, dumping the baggage of opinions—so that his burden grows lighter and lighter until it disappears entirely.

By racing wildly we lose ground and by simplifying and preparing we pull ahead. In a sense all work in the Dhamma is preparatory: we are working with our own minds; we prepare ourselves to understand what passes through our senses. Indolence and agitation are off the shoulders of the road, and our way lies between, where we should travel with due speed, but judiciously. Like horses, our enthusiasms need direction: it is fine to urge them on, but it is advisable to keep hold of the reins.

The benefits of Dhamma practice may appear quickly but still not be recognized because of their quiet, subtle nature. The practitioner may not be able to measure neatly his advance from one stage to another, but he may sense gradual, momentous changes in himself:

Just as a carpenter or a carpenter's assistant sees on his adze-handle the marks made by his fingers and thumb, but does not thereby have the knowledge, "So much of the adze-handle was worn away by me today, so much yesterday, so much at another time," but merely has the knowledge that it is being worn away by its wearing-away—In the same way, monks, a monk living devoted to the practice of mind-development does not have the knowledge, "So much of the taints was worn away today, so much yesterday, so much at another time." But he has the knowledge they are being worn away by their wearing away.

(Saṃyutta Nikāya XXII, 101)

One benefit of the Dhamma is the sense of direction and purpose that comes into daily life. Whereas before we may have been lurching between occupations and diversions with little hope or conviction, we now find that we have, however tenuously, connected ourselves with something higher and truer. Perhaps we could not give an exact account of it, but we sense that our time spent in study and meditation is a piece of life well worked, a field fairly sown, and that we have begun to apply our energies rightly.

Another benefit, another mark of progress, is the tendency to explore and investigate more than before. We want to know for ourselves; we are less willing merely to receive and react to information. Progress can also be noted in increased attention to and awareness of the causes and results of our intentional actions. We might see, for instance, how a mental state of anger, when unchecked, gives rise to intemperate words that annoy others, who then retaliate against us, causing pain and resentment and a hundred other ricocheting effects not soon controlled. Consequently, respect for the moral precepts increases as we recognize their value in protecting us from our foolish cravings and reflexes. We grow more conscious not only of what should be avoided but of what should be done, as in generosity, helpfulness, and pity for suffering beings.

Then there is the progress that is nothing grander than the more intimate, more precise knowledge of our own minds, with all their weaknesses. How could we heal ourselves if we did not see our wounds? A carefully acquired knowledge of how we fail or fall short corrects misunderstanding, deflates the swelling of conceit, and shows us our actual situation without the frightful shadows of imagination. With such daylight knowledge we may become braver, able to look upon the maelstrom of suffering without running away.

The Buddha taught that all worldly things are caused and conditioned. The practice of Dhamma sets up favorable conditions of virtue, concentration, and understanding that, besides leading on toward enlightenment, help us here and now in dealing with troubles and fears. Knowing the mind—be it scared or confident, shaken or calm—allows us to recognize and employ its powers for the good.

Finally, we may see progress in the growth of faith, even in the frailest green shoot out of the ground of a weary heart. What kind of faith? Just the small bloom of gladness over what we have done, the honest effort we have made—the faint smile of the spirit that begins to answer the Buddha's smile, the hopeful, wondering, peaceful feeling which we cannot well explain, which perhaps we cannot speak of at all except to murmur to ourselves, "This Dhamma is a good thing!"

None of these signs of progress are very startling, and the inattentive might miss them, become discouraged, and wander away in doubt. But with a proper understanding of the gradual, organic nature of the Dhamma this will not happen. Do we long for release from our woes and cares? Do we aspire to *Nibbāna*, the end of suffering? This goal, transcendent as it is, can be reached by the persevering. Even though our confidence and energy do not yet cut like lightning through all difficulties, we might see at least what we did not see before—that we live in *this* condition and have *that* yet to attain.

Let us reflect: why did the Buddha, standing alone in sublime completeness, decide to teach others? Could he not perceive the flagrant weaknesses of humanity? Could he not notice how quickly we tire, how slowly we understand, how miserably we excuse ourselves? We must suppose he could. Why then did he reveal the majestic Dhamma? It might be—indeed, it seems quite likely—that the Buddha himself had confidence, even in erring men and women. And certainly he had compassion. There is, we must remember, that smile of his, that ineffable smile that has stayed so vivid through history, that subtle curve of the lips on the statues and effigies of the master, that gentle, timeless, profound smile of enlightenment. Should we not then take heart, and by our faith and practice do at least some small homage to the great sage who did not refuse to help us? It matters less where we have been than where we are now and where we shall direct our steps. Treasuring some breath of wonder, some blossom of truth, some tender, newborn hope, we have come out of the badlands and climbed onto the upland trail. The horizon runs out to unknown immensities. Yesterday's camp lies far behind. The journey will continue, but we sleep tonight in a new country, under a clean sky, beneath the smile of the Buddha.

16. Reading the News

$\mathbb{R}$ THIS MORNING THE SUNDAY NEWSPAPER lies before us
on the porch, heavy, important, peremptory—as if demanding to be
picked up. From habit, almost from duty, we obey, sighing in expectation of the stark symbols that will jump into our eyes with their messages of new things happening: war, strife, crime, laughter, and pathos.
The headlines will draw us to the columns underneath that will relate
the stories born in only these last few hours. How can so much be
going on? Every day the fast world spins off this abundance, this sur-
feit, of news, and we have agreed, it seems, to pack our heads with it,
to exclaim over reported novelties, to repeat them to others, and to
treat them, for lack of anything better, as the newest and most significant facts of our shared experience.

But now the newspaper, cold and solemn, remains unopened and
heavy on our hands, and unaccountably some quirk of thought, some
mood of rebelliousness, moves us to set it aside. We eye it doubtfully,
wondering how long we can resist it. The day might prove tedious
with our curiosity unsated. But let us anyway slip out for a walk, postponing the attack of news, turning our steps toward the boundary of
the neighborhood to seek worthier intelligence or only silence.

Today reveals, perhaps, no special wonders of nature, no prodigies
of beauty. The sun keeps close within its cloudy quarters, and a breeze,
indifferently cold, loafs through the naked trees and swings a few

withered leaves. We are rambling through early spring, moving briskly enough, getting the blood circulating. The attention of the great world with its reporters and news organizations roves elsewhere, and we go unnoticed. To clear our heads we plod out here and veer away from houses, in search of solitude. Across a road and a hundred yards up a little valley of oaks and beeches, the swish of traffic begins to break down, dwindling behind us—mere strings of sound unraveling—less significant, finally, than the crunch of our shoes over sticks. We pick our way up a path alongside a shallow, unremarkable stream while two crows, far away, squawk in gloomy antiphony. If anything is happening in the world, we think, it is happening behind us. Ahead, the empty woods blur into a neutral mist.

But solitude is its own event. Our breathing deepens as the traffic sounds disappear. Our legs swing and our arms brush back the green arcs of brambles. We stoop and straighten, making our way deliberately. This is a little-traveled path, one that must be broken through with some attention to the entangling thorns; so exertion is called for and, being called, reminds us there is a physical body here which is doing our will. The body hitches, puffs, and flexes according to its nature, while the mind cranks away on its nebulous constructions, the two together in amazing cooperation for the continuance of life. Here in the damp quiet of the woods we begin to feel the links between body and mind, between memory and emotion, between intention and action. Cut off for now from the news, from the racket of civilization, we start to notice a network of causes and effects, seeing as from a distance this strange, composite person still staggering hopefully after an ideal.

We follow patterns—we are patterns—and when we are not venting opinions and commentary we might possibly trace the mystery of these patterns. We like to think ourselves original and special but, taking an objective view, what is really here except a handful of elements rolling like marbles in a box? The daily news and all our current worries only give the box a shake. The newness we admire and celebrate, then, must be deceptive; it is simply change and more change—a rearrangement, an endless alternation of gain and loss, repute and disrepute, praise and blame, happiness and suffering.

Now the path crosses the stream, where icy water slips over gray and white pebbles with a trickling sound that is not unpleasant. We pause. Here is something happening, after all. We stand frowning absurdly at it: a human being pondering a creek—one small commotion confronting another. In the pelting of sensation and the drone of news that make up our lives we find it hard to slow down enough to observe as a contemplator ought to observe, and in odd moments like this when we really want to understand what life is all about we find ourselves staring impatiently at this or that stone or sunset as if to demand, "Well, what is the *meaning* here?" But stones and sunsets and trickling streams have their own business to take care of—they go on changing like everything else—and they do not volunteer proverbs. Even if we had the patience to wait for a colossal revelation, would we recognize it if it came?

The best nature can do for us is to show us simple truth, to show us ourselves, to display the mental and the material, so that if we are ready we might see through the flashy wraps of concepts and conceits. Who or what is this curious person who anxiously guesses at the world? Whose ears register the running snow-melt? Who, if anyone, experiences the sound? If we spend time just watching out here in a forgotten place we might get an inkling. Like an expensive wristwatch laid on a tree stump, we feel oddly vulnerable away from our sofas— just a hot little whirring in the greater stillness. Are we ever wholly at ease with mind and body? Surely we have been too infatuated with a dubious arrangement: ramshackle limbs wobbling along, senses popping, mind distractedly chirping, a hundred volitions scrabbling for control.

We leap (or mind-and-body leaps) across the creek and trudge deeper into the unpromising woods, where sensation rakes us like little thorns, until we wonder if it might be good to stop interpreting and just let the world come and go in watchful peace. In this play of life, actors gesture and declaim, banners wave, the scenery slides and changes. Oh yes, there is a lot happening in the unleafed, muddy woods, and if we refrain from snatching at it we might learn something. After the freezes, thaws, and storms of winter the trees seem strangely graceful and portentous. Change happens when we are not looking. Sand and mud have washed over the path in places; a section of creek bank has collapsed; dead branches have fallen and cluttered the ground. Everywhere we find crisscrossing old logs sinking a little further into the earth, while above them stand the little saplings. Crows flap and quarrel in the distance. Somewhere a woodpecker taps out odd fragments of time. These things compose the present reality and deserve our thoughtful attention.

Our love of novelty is an expression of our endless wanting and also an evasion of the overwhelming impermanence of the world—an attempt to enjoy and discard each bright prize before time spoils it, to jump toward each promising spark and, landing, instantly get ready to jump again. We addict ourselves to distractions in order to avoid worrying about what lies beneath—the unexplained ferment of appearing and disappearing formations. Although we would *like* to be at peace, we continue to rush to momentary excitements, because we suspect that the attainment of peace would require the overthrow of our habits and a confrontation with unbearable fears. Certainly, real improvement in our lives can only come about through strong effort directed at the unwholesome roots of action, which are greed, hatred, and delusion, but at the same time the doubts that hold us back are weaker than they seem. The mind has closed the links of fear, and the mind can cut them.

The ancient and continuing experience of travelers on the path of Dhamma is that the effort to get free puts new, encouraging light in the gloomy regions of the mind. Like a gold thread glinting in a tapestry, the theme of joy runs through Buddhist history—not only joy in the final victory but even in the beginning stages of Buddhist practice when life, long a patchwork of guesses, begins to acquire a purpose. The first disciples of the Buddha were not morose, groaning hermits; they were vigorous people, rejoicing in the work they were doing, congratulating each other on their good fortune, elated to find that the worst of the contemplative life was in the dread of coming face to face with their ignorance, and that the actual experience was bracing and inspiring. After listening to the Buddha's discourses they were gladdened; when they went away to meditate they were determined. So it was through the ages, when accumulating sorrows and questions drove seekers away from the futility of the passions and toward that inspection of reality that is the road to liberation. Turning to the ageless Dhamma, they lost their taste for puerile novelty and their fear of chaos underneath. The puzzle of life engaged them fully, and they were the happier for it. They heard the news worth hearing and, in the profoundest sense, informed themselves.

To go sauntering in these woods or anywhere is no real achievement even if—especially if—we are on the lookout for marvels. A grasping mind is no prettier here than in the roaring city. When we walk we do best not to hunt for unusual objects, for scenic trinkets, but just to know whatever comes before us, be it acorns or toadstools or ice in a footprint. If, as the Buddha teaches, all phenomena bear the three characteristics of existence—impermanence, unsatisfactoriness, and nonself—we ought to be able to relax our preferences—for indeed, inconstant and uncertain as we are, how should we choose our own inspirations?

So let us go on with mindfulness ready for the ordinary, in a wakeful silence. The leisurely path winds on through the woods until we find it blocked, here, by a fallen tree, not the first we have stepped over, but one worth noting because—even to our unpracticed eyes it is obvious—it is newly fallen. That living and dead trees blow down does not surprise us; that such wrecks mark the forest as far as we can see is only natural; that all life comes to term and passes is a truism. Why then do we not throw a leg over this obstacle and be on our way? Perhaps we pause because the fractured trunk, the broken boughs, the crushed shrubs beneath, and the torn-up earth together tell us that this event has *just* happened, maybe within this day or this hour, and that the solid background of our existence has suffered a wound and is no longer what it was.

The tree has been uprooted, yielding to wind or disease or the weakness of age. We peer into the crater at its base. We stare at the tangle of broken roots jutting into the air and still gripping great rocks. With rot at its core, the tree might have been already half dead. It had to fall, of course, sometime, but is it not still shocking that it did so now? Ailing or well, it stood for decades until out of the inscrutable processes of cause and effect there came the circumstances to knock it

149

down. Beholding now the cracked bark and the rotted, weakened trunk, we can only nod and acknowledge that it had to be, imagining the awesome seconds when it pitched out of the sky and smashed a throng of saplings. Here, surely, is news.

But where are the reporters and the photographers and the marveling crowds? Is this not an epochal change? Should it not sober thinking persons to see that even the long-lived must meet destruction at last, that immemorial endurance has a limit, that something in the cells, in the molecules, in the mighty river of natural law overturns everything that has grown up? Mountains wash away, suns go out, the lone daisy withers in a glass on a table—and we, likewise ephemeral, have not understood. Now the news strikes fresh upon us and we must feel its powerful resonance. Thinking, watching, trying intermittently to comprehend, we have lived pressing toward the future. Maybe we should turn, instead, to study the nature of falling trees, so we do not get crushed beneath them.

No cameras, no reporters on these premises. Only a gray squirrel on the overhanging branch of a nearby tree laconically comments on the devastation, which is ancient and new, routine and stunning—another jolt in the cosmic unrest. The squirrel clucks and clicks with an eye toward us. What obsequies would suit for a fallen tree? What eulogy could we pronounce? We do not know. And meanwhile all other elements of impetuous nature, titanic and minute, race on through the drama of arising, persisting, and passing away, heedlessly hurrying on and on. No time to notify the news people. No time to ponder the past. No time at all that we can catch hold of and clasp to ourselves.

And yet the news has got out. The universal situation has been declared by the Buddha: "All formations are impermanent." Who has heard this, really heard it? Who has fitted the thought to experience and felt the current of truth gush through him? Have we? Or have we only imagined? Have we crouched in our dim doubts, affrighted and diverted by trifles only, all our lives long? A fresh intelligence, always in season, ripens like fruit on every bush, and the Buddha announces it, points it out, and extols its sweetness, but the reaching and the harvesting must be our own great task.

So maybe we pause to muse; maybe we sit right down on the rough trunk of this toppled tree and ease back our straining after knowledge. If we attend seriously to the words of the Buddha, and if we stay alert to impressions on our senses, watching and noting the repetition of patterns, then we may hope that intuition will awake in us and mature into wisdom. Insight into impermanence, unsatisfactoriness, and non-self is not accidental; we cannot create it, either; but we can make possible its birth by setting up favorable conditions, by training ourselves in mindfulness and bearing down with concentration. Instructive trees will then grow up directly before us. We do not need to chase after unknown truth so much as to restrain our own conduct and widen our view to be ready for whatever significant thing that might appear—and significant things are always appearing.

Here before us in the cold air some kind of tiny insect hovers, terribly early for the season, it seems, mysteriously arisen from its icy sleep and drifting away unguessably to death or survival. The newspapers have missed the story, but we must not. Underfoot, the first sprouts are already breaking the forest floor—who would have suspected it? Who would have suspected his own mind to be a stream of processes as ownerless as the woodland rills? But this is what we find when we subdue our mental commentary for a time and watch what sensations write on the screen of consciousness. We have much in common, it seems, with creeks and trees and clouds. These events are current and invite investigation.

Our seat is damp; the day is damp. The body pulls attention to itself again, shivering, and we have to respond, to get moving, to take up our duties. But if tree or stream or insect has launched an uncommon thought, if our minds sail for a moment on a new course, shall we not suppose that a grand quest is indeed possible for us, or has already begun?

Let us go on then, mindfully and deliberately. The day is not finished yet and many truths await our recognition and faith. So, down another path and on through weeds and briars and across a road, we return from the forest to that other forest of society with, let us hope, our habits shoved askew and our minds made ready.

And now, here we stand once again on warm carpets in the domain of radio, television, and newspapers, where we are ambushed by sight and sound, where information swirls around us like smoke. But we do not, after all, have to be captivated. Impressions on our senses arouse certain kinds of consciousness, but we need not pounce on any of them. We can survey them mindfully, applying ourselves to what is useful, letting pass what is not, listening meanwhile to the deeper communication of the running moment. The furnace clicks in the basement; voices echo and murmur; the cat in the armchair blinks at us and counts off eternity in the flicks of her tail. All formations are impermanent. What then have we been holding on to? Wonderfully, bulletins fall thick upon us—like snowflakes on a pond, like rain on oak leaves. The story is illustrated. The news has got out and has reached us, who have the chance to understand.

17. *Death and Chrysanthemums*

🍃 THE VISITOR TO A BUDDHIST TEMPLE will likely find flowers in the shrine room. People bring them to beautify the place, to honor the Buddha, and perhaps to demonstrate something in their hearts that cannot well be said in words. Sometimes these are cut flowers that sweeten the air of the shrine for a while, and sometimes they are blooming, potted plants with foliage and flowers that last a little longer, until lack of light or just the cycles of nature cause them to fade and wilt. Then they get carried outside to be discarded, or perhaps to be planted whole somewhere in the garden, or to be taken away if somebody wants them. The rotation continues, so that some freshness and color might always grace the temple. Once the flowers have passed their peak and have been removed, no one gives them any thought. Or, it may be, none but those really keen on making an end of suffering.

May we invite you, neighbor, out here to the back yard to inspect some dying flowers? Do not plead other duties, other places to go. In our cyclic journeys we are all going to this contemplation eventually; let us learn the territory. These plants are chrysanthemums, you can see, quite finished as to beauty, dying back fast now, irreversibly decaying in the usual way. After a few days of loveliness the yellow flowers show a brown stain, then a swift curling and drooping, while the leaves shrink as from an invisible fire. What fire? We might say, the fire of impermanence, ardently eating up the marrow of the world. It smolders here in these sorry stalks, in these collapsing blooms, and even—disconcertingly, now that we look—even in the hands we extend to turn the pot. All these marks and scars and blemishes—testimonies of years and worlds gone by.

When we gaze long on chrysanthemums or any dear and lovely thing, do we not feel sometimes, even in our pleasure, the obscure anxiety, the foreshadowing of their passing? But is it not curious how we cannot explain what exactly is beauty, or what exactly is the peak or prime of any object we admire? "Flower" is a word pasted over just one phase of a process that we find most pleasing. Out of a crowd of conditions of soil, water, sun, and seed, the clenched bud rises, slowly widening a yellow eye; then the unfurling petals, the young bloom, the broader flower, then the stain creeping into the yellow, the shriveling and steady desolation. No period in the cycle is possible without the others. Conditions follow one another as continuously as water flowing.

These potted flowers, given the inscrutable ways of chrysanthemums, may die back to the dirt but for a stalk or two, perhaps to put forth new shoots in time, perhaps not. In their present state they are repulsive, which is why they get banished to the back yard—and why we banish them and their symbolism from our minds as well, wishing to dwell always with the pleasant. But such a dwelling is, as we nevertheless know, quite unattainable; so the longing for permanence and the fact of death saw back and forth painfully on our minds.

Come now, neighbor, crouch down here and admire these derelict flowers. Color changes, texture changes, shape changes, and have ever done so. We would stop the decay if we could, but we cannot, and even if we could we know it would be folly. Imagine these flowers daubed with varnish, stiff as wires, lit with spotlights and soaked with perfume—a poor imposture that could not please us much. We would know that vitality had fled. No, there is no help for it—what we care for changes and vanishes even as we cling, and in the clinging there is grief.

Now, it may be that we have just attended—or will soon attend, so certain is nature—the funeral of someone we loved: a ritual with flowers in abundance as if to drive back sorrow with massed loveliness.

That dear and irreplaceable person is gone, and pain diffuses through the void in our hearts. Always in our grief, in our fear of grief, we want some counterpoise to death, some protest or denial of its finality. This is natural and customary and human, but it is also unavailing. Might there be another way to tranquility? Have we ever stepped past the casket to meditate on the arrayed flowers in their own swift, silent passage to age and dissolution? All things from ocean foam to galaxies preach Dhamma when the mind grows still and listens. Seed, root, stalk, and flower—on they roll, and on rolls the whole wheel of conditioned existence, ensuring pleasure and pain, elation and sorrow, as long as the constituent elements stay glued together. And with what glue but clinging? There cannot be birth without death or death without birth while we cling. There cannot be these lilies and carnations without the wilting of lilies and carnations.

We cling to the phases of brightness and get pulled into the darkness again and again. But if this is so, as we can hardly doubt, should we then subsist without flowers or love in a moribund universe, forever grimly intent on decay? A bitter cure for grief! But such is not the way of the Buddha. Rather, this death or any death should motivate us to contemplate and come to terms with the wheel of *saṃsāra*, and then to transcend it.

All compounded things have the characteristics of arising and ceasing—not only people and flowers. So distressing is this fact—or rather the suspicion of this fact, until we comprehend it in experience—that the frightened mind retreats to delusions of permanence, security, and well-being, much as a passenger in an airplane might pull down his window shade and pretend he is sitting perfectly still in a motionless room. But this is only a temporary, unsustainable fiction. In our own daily lives, doubtful, apprehensive, wearied with amusements, we cannot go on forever believing in security and permanence. The walls of not-seeing, not-looking, not-believing crack and fall to shocks, calamities, or the slow crush of time. Then pain pours in, made worse by the seeming pointlessness of it all.

The Buddhist solution to the problem is to break down the walls of delusion before great trials strike, or even to use such trials as a tool to pry open the locks of fear. In Buddhism we find no false comfort, no tiptoeing around the unpleasantness of death. In the absence of wisdom, death is indeed a bad thing, not a sweet and certain transition to eternal heaven. It is a bad thing because it interrupts our efforts for emancipation and sends us spinning off to unknown rebirth, or sends our *minds* spinning off in sorrow when the death is our friend's. Death is a hard fact, an inescapable fact, and we have to consider it and know it for what it is.

But do we not already know what death is? Sadly, we do not. We think of it as a singular catastrophe that erases individual beings. Thus we dread it for years and weep when it strikes our loved ones, putting what looks like a total end to the existing person. Out of natural reflex we misapprehend both death and the one to whom it happens; but a systematic analysis of compounded things into their parts and conditions will lead to a different view. "Death," we come to realize, is a word fastened more or less haphazardly on experience without understanding of the whole underlying process, which is, at its simplest, just a relentless rising and falling of events, a coming into existence and a going out of existence, a perpetual flux. Human beings, dolphins, rocks, and trees suffer alike this elemental impermanence or instability, with their complex or primitive components coming into being, staying a while, then ceasing, passing away, making way for something else. If we are alert to changes we will be surprised to see that changes are happening all the time—countless drops that make up the flood of conditioned existence.

If we are *not* alert, however, and if we have no knowledge of the Dhamma, we are apt to fall into one of two extreme views very common in the world. On the one hand there is eternalism, the belief that this very person, self, or apparent ego will last, will continue, will be identifiably preserved after death in some form or other. On the other hand there is annihilationism, the belief that an existing person will be annihilated, destroyed at death, that with the destruction of the body a man or a woman is simply obliterated and is no more. Buddhism avoids both these wrong extremes by focusing on the essential process of existence, which is the interaction of self-less *conditions*. Life is a conditioned pattern, not a graspable *thing*. It is beginninglessly and endlessly renewed by ignorant craving, giving only the appearance, to our unenlightened eyes, of absolute "selves" traveling through time.

Death as we usually understand it—or misunderstand it—is inseparable from the concept of somebody or some entity who undergoes death. But Buddhism teaches that what we call a person is a combination of five impermanent, conditioned aggregates or groups: material form or body; pleasant, unpleasant, and neutral feeling; perception; mental formations or activities; and consciousness. These aggregates act together in intricate combination to give the appearance of an enduring personality or ego, but this "person," while solid enough in a limited, ordinary sense, is not solid in the ultimate sense. Here we have another concept stretched over usually misunderstood natural phenomena. The Buddha explains:

> *Suppose, monks, a large lump of froth was floating on this river Ganges and a clear-sighted man were to see it, observe it, and properly examine it. Seeing it, observing it, properly examining it, it would appear to him to be empty, unsubstantial, without essence. What essence, monks, could there be in a lump of froth?*

> *In the same way, monks, whatsoever body...feeling...perception...mental activities...consciousness, past, future, or present, internal or external, gross or subtle, inferior or superior, far or near, that a monk sees, observes, and properly examines...it would appear to him to be empty, unsubstantial, without essence. What essence, monks, could there be in body...in feeling...in perception...in mental activities...in consciousness?*
> (Saṃyutta Nikāya XXII, 95)

Any aspect of the mind and body complex, when shrewdly investigated, reveals itself to be merely a perishable part, not an essence. When we can find nowhere a center or core but only transient, interdependent parts, we are obliged to consider that what we witness and experience and attach a name to is a profoundly unsubstantial flux of causality—events springing from causes and giving rise to further events. This is not to say that everything is imaginary, or that we do not exist—rather that we do not exist in the way we think we do, but as the dynamic, ever-changing result of innumerable conditions. Such an understanding of the made-up, compounded "individual" must, therefore, alter our view of the death of the individual. What sort of end can this be? From the highly personal destruction of a self, we come down to the dispersal of essence-less factors. Where there is no firm ground, only floating bubbles, where shall we fling ourselves down, how shall we begin our mourning? Death, in the elemental sense of falling after rising, is going on all the time, all throughout any given life, so the physical death of the body should be seen as one more change in the ancient process.

We might say with some logic that death is thus a normal state of affairs and offers little reason for clinging and grieving. Still, of course, we *do* grieve, and rare is the bereaved person who is consoled by logic alone. The beauty of Buddhist teaching, however, is that it grows from the ground of reason, preparing the mind and dispelling false notions, and blossoms into the fragrant, liberating experience of the truth. How? As we have suggested—by widening our view until we can appreciate more than one thin segment of reality. When the follower of Dhamma has come to see, with immediate and tremendous clarity, that there is in fact nothing of substance in this foam of change, internally or externally, that can be clung to, then the question of trying to cling simply can no longer come up. With the cessation of ignorance there comes the cessation of craving for the impossible, and with the cessation of craving there comes the blessed cessation of suffering. With no more fire the overwrought heart cools.

If we can gradually train our minds to see what the Buddha teaches, and what in fact all of nature shows, then we can approach that cessation, that glorious liberation. Not only have we long misunderstood the nature of ourselves and others, but with our narrow view we have lamented death as an *end*. Yet the five aggregates that make up the person cannot strictly be said to "end" at death or to "begin" at birth because they themselves have never been subsisting, enduring entities at all—only groups or streams of conditioned events that continually arise and break up and arise again. When the body dies the material basis on which the living process depends is lost, but as long as the current of energy lasts—as long as ignorance and craving keep churning—

there can be no finality or rest. The cooperative process of the aggregates continues. Out of the momentum of built-up *kamma*, rebirth takes place in an appropriate new organism, in this world or another. No self expires; no self passes on. One life causes and conditions its successor, much as the vibration in one section of a wire fence jumps into the next section, perpetuating a visible pattern. Ordinarily we say, correctly, that a person dies and takes rebirth elsewhere according to his or her deeds; but in stricter, philosophical terms we can say that no one dies and no one is born—phenomena just repeatedly arise out of conditions.

There is consolation here, if we take the time to let emotions settle. When loved ones die we should remember that this is not the absolute "end" of them, as it appears to our earthbound eyes, but that, until such time as they attain full enlightenment, they are set for rebirth, for new life, whose quality will be determined by the quality of their own deeds. A good person, one who has acted virtuously, has a happy destiny ahead, a fortunate result of *kamma*, in one or another of the many planes of existence. Moreover, this person was never as limited and defined as we thought. Our suffering now is the result of the ignorance and desire with which we looked at him or her. If we release this person from the framework of literal concepts we release ourselves as well from a painful prison. How could we hold in place that which is ever moving? How could we embrace forever five spinning, empty aggregates? Such a sorrowful error! How much better simply to love and let go.

Now, neighbor, would you not agree that these wasted chrysanthemums are not so ugly as we thought at first? Are they not instructive, ripe with Dhamma, even as they bend here insensately toward the earth? There is no cause for disgust, no need to hurry to the store for a fresh pot. Here are some green leaves remaining, sprung from the same roots. Even if there were not, the future of chrysanthemums is not depleted; somehow the seeds get around. Somehow the *kamma* of sentient beings gets around, too, uncountable in its risings, shaping birth upon birth.

And here we arrive at the crux of the problem. When we fear annihilation of our own or someone else's "self," we might take some reassurance from the Buddhist vision of repeated birth, which offers always a new chance, a new opportunity for wandering beings. But this is still a low plateau, for novices only, undependable on further inspection; we have to take another breath and resume the climb. The Buddha saw the fact of rebirth as another aspect of unsatisfactoriness. The sorrows of existence are not unique events; they go on happening again and again from limitless past to inconceivable future; if we adjust to this present decease, no matter—more are coming, and as long as we have not penetrated into an understanding of the selflessness of the aggregates, as long as we have not extinguished the defilements in our hearts and attained true security, more pains must come as well.

In the cycles of *saṃsāra*, in the conditioned succession of rebirths, good and virtuous beings certainly enjoy the happy results of their accumulated good deeds, finding havens of great peace and serenity. But even in the sublime, heavenly planes, we are told, life eventually reaches a limit, breaks down, comes to an end; and the unenlightened inhabitants of those lovely realms are necessarily scattered again like vagabonds with no inheritance or refuge but their own deeds. What should this suggest to a courageous thinker, who is aware of his weaknesses but aware also of his precious, momentary glimpse of Dhamma? The Buddha draws a challenging picture:

Inconceivable is the beginning of this saṃsāra; not to be discovered is a first beginning of beings who, obstructed by ignorance and ensnared by craving, are hurrying and hastening through this round of rebirths....

Long have you suffered the death of father and mother, of sons, daughters, brothers, and sisters. And whilst you were thus suffering, you have, indeed, shed more tears upon this long way than there is water in the four great oceans....

And thus, O monks, have you long undergone suffering, undergone torment, undergone misfortune, and filled the graveyards full; verily, long enough to be dissatisfied with all the forms of existence, long enough to turn away and free yourselves from them all.

(Saṃyutta Nikāya XV)

Such is the unflinching vision of the Buddha, who urges us on to *Nibbāna*, to liberation from the whole uproar of birth and death. We might forget death for a time, but we cannot evade the thought or the fact forever. Small respites will serve us only temporarily, only long enough for us to catch our breath, to get our feet under us once again. Behind us lie the tearful wastes we have journeyed in so long. Now we must make a new journey beyond them entirely.

We cannot escape suffering merely by dying, because rebirth follows, produced by our craving. This present life, with all its troubles, offers a wonderful opportunity for doing good work, achieving nobility of mind, and eliminating craving. Into this sphere of baffling contradictions the human being who was to become the Buddha was born, and here he realized supreme enlightenment, and here he announced the way to *Nibbāna*, teaching the incomparable Dhamma to relieve the sorrow of living beings. Here also is where we must practice, bravely bearing misfortunes, refraining from bad deeds, doing good deeds, striving to cleanse our hearts, conscientiously building our own characters. If we apply ourselves now to such tasks, working patiently, we will find our days wisely spent and our whole lives beautified with earned blessings.

The Buddha said that just as the ocean has only one taste, the taste of salt, so his teaching has only one taste, the taste of liberation. We, neighbor, squatting here in the warm sun, musing over chrysanthemums, begin to taste the Dhamma—a flavor not of tears and burning grief but of something unutterably fine and sweet and pure? It should move us to search for more goodness, to abandon more folly, to learn what should be learned.

By many similes the Buddha emphasized the precariousness and brevity of our worldly career and the *dukkha* within it. The diligent, who have devoted themselves to virtuous deeds and mental development, go on, inspired, to greater happiness, while the indolent wander woefully out of this life as ignorant as they came into it. Dreamers squander their advantages, their chances of making progress, by thinking lazily, "Oh, there is time, there is time." Time there may be; time there will *surely* be, in one world or another; but opportunity to learn there may not be.

The days and nights are flying past,
Life dwindles hurriedly away;
The life of mortals vanishes
Like water in a tiny stream.

(Saṃyutta Nikāya IV, 10)

Here is an opportunity, in reach of our senses, right in these disintegrating chrysanthemums. For even in these withered petals the Four Noble Truths themselves stand out, speaking here in the dialect of flowers. The truth of suffering is the loss, weakness, and wrongness inherent in conditioned things—the inability to keep off change and preserve what is dear. These yellow blossoms lose their strength; their beauty runs out; helplessly they decay. We cannot protect them; after a few days we sigh with regret. But what is the truth of the origin of our small suffering, our tiny disappointment here? It is only the old spur of craving, the urge to control the uncontrollable. Like the faces of our beloved relatives and friends these chrysanthemums must change and fall away. So we must turn for help to the truth of the cessation of suffering. If the craving itself can be demolished then the whole dependent mass of suffering, the round of pain, will come to an end. With no more futile lunging after this or that the mind will come to balance in freedom, liberation, peace, *Nibbāna*. The truth of the way to this cessation of suffering is as always the Noble Eightfold Path: right view, right intention, right speech, right action, right livelihood, right effort, right mindfulness, and right concentration. In the midst of birth and death this path teaches grace and calm when thinking, speaking, acting—when bearing away exhausted flowers.

We have sorrowed long enough and we have died long enough. The Dhamma is splendid beyond telling, balm to the hurt, tonic to the brave, lamp to the questing. Look up to the traveling sun, if you will, neighbor—the bright hour comes round; the noon of our strength is now. Stretch yourself as you will. What is left to say? Sermons are falling from the very air, numberless as flower petals.

18. Emblems of Dhamma

SOMEWHERE FAR FROM HERE a hundred little streams drop out of the hills and find each other in the valleys. Called a river then, and given a name, this community of waters meanders on to our city, widening, deepening, evolving, gathering into itself leaves, pollen, soil, seeds—rolling slow or fast with the shape of the land, glazed by sun and punctured by rain, drawn on to the namelessness of the ocean—a long blue and green metaphor where we sail our boats and our thoughts, and by whose shore our ancestors have stood and where our children too will stand, gazing and wondering.

Around here the river slips and spills through a mile or two of rapids and shallows before passing smoothly by the city. These turbulent reaches with their backwaters are the resort of fishermen, hikers, and (or so it is to be hoped) philosophers, because the river speaks Dhamma to those who approach with their hearts prepared. We can find solitude of a sort and a place for listening here in this strip of frequently inundated bottomland that lies still, uninviting and unbeautiful, under the glaring sun. Flat, broken, and swampy, too low to be built upon—at least by the builders of physical structures—it yet puzzles and intrigues by its very wildness. Let us go, then, let us cross it. Though the ground is rough and tangled for casual strollers, a band of blue water sparkles attractively in the distance, and if we must have a nameable destination for our walk that will do.

Over there, against the steep far bank, the river surges through its channel most of the year, though with the spring rains it engulfs the bottomland, tearing away the old debris and depositing the new. In the ravaged sycamores that survive here we can see, above our heads, wads of dead leaves and streamers of cloth or plastic, telling how high the last flood swelled. Wobbling on the stones and stranded driftwood, we look up, bemused, imagining walking beneath that torrent. Again and again the flood has come, remaking the boulder-field, and still some wretched, leaning trees live on, bushes flourish between the stones, and pools ripple with small life. We cannot help but notice a dumb persistence in nature, a rising-and-falling that causes us to wonder if we ourselves are persisting toward some good end or only rising and falling, drowning and reviving by turns.

To hike through this untidy bit of wilderness to the river's edge is not easy in the labyrinth of dense grass and boulders, but when, with sore ankles, we stumble down to rest by the spray at last, we feel our hearts bravely beating and know we have begun to earn the fruit of contemplation. Though jet airplanes thunder overhead now and then and cars glitter on a distant bridge, we have solitude enough, and the wide earth opens to our view.

This scene is not entirely charming, though it has a grandeur we might profitably explore. Down here away from the city the winds rock to and fro; the river plunges and hisses; green hills fade away into a vacant sky. It is summer now, and the boulders burn against our skin as we sit and blink in the harsh glare of the high sun. Time hardly matters here where centuries roll by like birds lazily gliding at the zenith. Winter or stormy autumn would be no prettier, surely, with icy water mindlessly driving on. In all seasons there is mud and washed-up refuse. But as philosophers should we not extend ourselves beyond mere appearances? If so we must make our inchoate longings for understanding condense to attentiveness and observation. By exerting ourselves we can see what there is to see.

Too often we suck up experience like a drug and swish it in our minds to savor its pleasure. The superficial lover of nature is out simply to *please* himself, and though that is not necessarily bad, neither is it praiseworthy or productive. One thing every student of Dhamma should come to realize is that pleasures of the senses fail quickly and give no real sustenance; so when we behold the spectacle of the charging river let us not be slack, but instead meditate upon these mingled elements of light, foam, sound, smell, rock, and water. If they are beautiful to us that is no great matter. What do they signify? And beyond significance, what are they in themselves?

If we stay a while listening to the multitudinous speech of the water we are apt to be teased out of ourselves and swung here and there in the play of nature, mesmerized by the green current, lulled by the windy spaces around us. But let us not be too docile. What is really going on here? What mood dominates? Surely we must feel the immense age of this earth, its endless, weary metamorphosis. The boulders we perch our ephemeral bodies on are remnants of ancient plains and mountains. The river, frisking with deceptive youth, has been wearing at the layered rock past human memory, finding its way down through the bluffs to its present level. There is an epic sameness and soberness in the history written in stone. What remains of any worldly works? The earth itself is here being transformed, cracking and falling, undercut by a slippery nothing of water. The summer's curling vine explores the face of the eroding cliff; tiny creatures twitch in the rain-pockets in rock; and everything goes on changing under the changing sky. So the emblem of impermanence rises to our minds, and we are forced to contemplate our own vulnerable skin and fluttering breath. With the roots of mountains washing away before us, how preposterous is our shrill vanity, and how much a glimpse of Dhamma shakes us. We live scampering between floods; surely we cannot afford to build with straws anymore.

The river is now blue, now green, now white in the rapids. Supple and shifting, it dazzles us. We might call it beautiful, but faced with all this change, this unrest, we grow tired even of beauty and long to find an ultimate serenity beyond all commotion. Shall we walk on? Down here beneath the notice of the great world we make our way, our small way, through the landscape of emblems. The bushes and grass and weeds that survive here pinched between the rocks impart a green haze to the flood plain, or in the winter a tawny blur. Bugs and butterflies are born from cocoons in the twigs. Things condition one another and make up the shimmering world we perceive in any moment. At our approach frightened ducks in the swamps and backwaters bolt into the air, excitedly gabbling, and wheel in huge circles overhead, then drop and settle again nearby—as if in search of safer quarters but unable to break the habit that holds them to their uncertain sanctuary. Crows and gulls, too, flap and glide and cry out their untranslatable desires, while far above the jets rumble.

But we cannot stare mindlessly, because walking requires care and balance, up and down stone slabs and through impeding grass and mud and around pools of water. In hiking along, beginning to perspire, we find that the day has a rough sufficiency that is fairly pleasant to think about. Might this be enough to live on? Though we are mortal creatures, could we just forget our problems by identifying ourselves—somehow—with this austere wasteland, this great and seemingly immortal river, this bird-decorated sky? Further along the bank we pass a few silent fishermen with rods and nets. We pause, squinting in the sun, as a fish is landed, flapping and twisting. The fisherman seizes it, patiently pries the hook out of the throat, and dumps the catch into a bucket. Was that a streak of blood we saw? Onward a little further, we are startled by the stench of something dead. Fish guts on the rocks. No need to look too closely; a glance over there is enough, we decide, moving away hastily, thinking better of identifying ourselves with river valleys or anything. But already scales and flesh and a cloud of flies make up an emblem of unsatisfactoriness—even while the river frolics and the sweet blue sky floats overhead.

Life catches us with bewildering contradictions. Joys are bitten by frost and griefs are softened by springtime. This plane of existence shows such an ambivalent character that a human being is driven to surrender to confusion or melancholy or, less commonly, to pursue a pilgrimage to awakening. And how brave are we today, how intent on awakening? Are we tired of dreaming? Can we contemplate what swings right before us now?

We blink until the too-bright scene becomes clear. Here is something hideous, out of place, suspended from a sapling. It jolts our senses for a second before we can interpret it: a small fish, dead, some six inches long, dried to a nasty figure of decay, dangling from a length of transparent line. Who put it here? It sways and turns, grossly dead, mummified and disgusting, with an eye or the shrunken pit of an eye staring out with infinite bleakness at us and all things. The harmony of the valley dies in that awful eye, and at once we turn away our own eyes and look around for something green and gentle. But in doing so do we not betray ourselves? For must not the real philosopher, the seeker, confront all forms that appear, not just the beautiful?

So let us meet with a ready mind this emblem of Dhamma that has shocked us. It signifies death, of course, the rude breakup of vitality and gladness. It warns that time is short for living beings; it mocks us with its swimming in air, suggesting the empty flurry of our busyness. So much for symbolism. Here the recreational philosopher might break off his pondering, but the follower of Dhamma must go on. Things present aspects of beauty or ugliness to us that we can and should read, but these are only the outward spoor of truth, which the wise have declared to dwell right here in our own minds and bodies. The fish offends and troubles us with its message of decay, but the anxiety is our own, made out of our fear and ignorance. We might take a lesson of death, but not gladly; we might take it as a hint to hurry even more to *accomplish* things, to experience more of what is considered pleasurable, but we are not the happier for it. This empty knot of aggregates we call "I" writhes with passion and prejudice, and it seems so hard ever to be free of them, and indeed we are afraid to be free of them. Yet the little fish here, irresistibly pulling our gaze, is more than an emblem; it is a fact as the boulders and the grass are facts; it is a shout of reality; it is a vessel of knowledge.

If we stand eye to eye with it, unrecoiling, and let our thought bore in, what do we see? What does contemplation discover? Beneath the grotesque form there is just the dried remainder of skin and flesh, beneath them a tiny tree of bone. There are shape and consistency that somehow make a fish a fish. And what beneath? Only finer and finer webs and bits of mysterious matter, gossamer patterns, sparks of being in endless change. In silence the imagination sails into space, elements, gulfs between stars. Where has death gone to, where has ugliness gone to? If we raise our own hand, our beloved and familiar hand, we discern the lines, pores, blemishes, crevices, and canyons of a strange and boundless country. Where does it end and where does our mortal beauty go? All earthly experience is made of changing formations: the anxious, circling ducks, the lifeless fish, the flowering weeds, our own flesh and dreams. They resolve to echoing space, emptiness, immeasurable oceans, and—strange to tell—no one hides inside. Within the solid, within the terrifying or the lovely, there is found only the slow, swinging bell of nonself, heard only by the contemplator.

With a mind alert and still we can know the world without liking or disliking, without distraction. If we faintly perceive even in a dangling fish the marks of existence we can begin to shed our own accustomed suffering, because suffering depends on craving and clinging, on the myth that there is something that can be clung to. When the myth dissolves, what shall remain to torment us? Truly our lives are temporary constructions, limited and conditioned by the law of change, and yet the more we realize this the nearer we approach liberation. Pain arises from longing for a worldly permanence that does not exist, and if we experience this truth we can begin to let go, diminish pain, and open the dimension of the timeless.

To be secure is not to command talent, wealth, adoration, or power, but to be attuned to the state of the universe as it is. All things in this river valley and in the world beyond run on in their cycles without rest, ever rolling. Yet there is a freedom possible, and this is what should engage our minds in this vital flicker of eternity. Our bones will build the cliffs of the future and we will be reborn high or low again, but what will that avail us if we become no wiser or better? Shall we not aim for wisdom and earn emancipation? The rest is flotsam in the endless stream.

The dry little fish turns on its line in the wind, and its eye sweeps over us and all formations—milder now, it seems. Time to move on, then, wherever we will. So let us go, now that our breath flows free again, now that the wind has come up in the scraggly trees. Let us go on in today's adventure, high-stepping through the deep grass and skirting the swamps and clambering over driftwood, while above us the jets strain toward heaven. Now we stride and hop, trip and recover, making our way in the direction we have chosen; and now we balance on a spine of rock, looking to the blue zenith, and for a moment hold the body in equilibrium. But have we yet set our minds in equilibrium, steady on the even way? We are walking, but have we got beyond yesterday's ignorance?

Now, as if we followed the arc of a stone thrown high in the sun-flooded air, we let our gaze fall from sky and trees down to the earth before us. *Here.* Here in this random day in eternity, here in the soft ground between the rocks we see, of all strange signs and symbols, the unmistakable hoofprint of a deer, and further along a cluster of others, among cans and bottles and scraps of plastic, here in the rank mud of this suburban valley. Amazingly a few deer survive in the poor thickets of the riverbank and boulder-field. Is this not testimony to the inexhaustible springs of life and will? Might we not drink at those springs and fortify our hearts to attempt what we only timidly dream of? Surely more revelations await us. Struck sharp and deep in the changeable mud, momentarily present for our momentary vision, a single hoofprint, a letter from the universal alphabet, illustrates the Dhamma, that which is to be seen by the focused mind. And now the scent of the earth rises around us like incense, and now if we have ears for it the jets are making a brave thunder, and the river is chanting pure doctrine, and above in the leaning trees the plastic shreds are blowing and exulting like flags. Can it be after all that we live in a holy country?

Impermanence, unsatisfactoriness, nonself. First we read the message in characters of ink or stone or earth and then see through them—know through them—toward the radiant reality beyond all places. There is no need to run after the marvelous, the plain scene of any moment being fruitful enough when we walk the good path· of Dhamma through city or country. We should not despise the light on chrome or the rust trailing down from a nail in a wall, any more than a budding wildflower. Truth shows through all faces of nature. To perceive what is needful we have nothing but these frail senses, but they are sufficient if we direct them wisely. Then we have reason for faith. The river will flow on, the deer may live and prosper, and the ducks may fly out of the valley at last.

Index

Page numbers in boldface refer to definitions.

About Wisdom Publications

WISDOM PUBLICATIONS is dedicated to offering works relating to and inspired by Buddhist traditions.

To learn more about us or to explore our other books, please visit our website at www.wisdompubs.org. You can subscribe to our e-newsletter or request our print catalog online, or by writing to:

Wisdom Publications
199 Elm Street
Somerville, Massachusetts 02144 USA

You can also contact us at 617-776-7416, or info@wisdompubs.org.

Wisdom is a nonprofit, charitable 501(c)(3) organization, and donations in support of our mission are tax deductible.

Wisdom Publications is affiliated with the Foundation for the Preservation of the Mahayana Tradition (FPMT).

Other Books by Bhikkhu Nyanasobhano

Longing for Certainty
Reflections on the Buddhist Life

Available Truth
Excursions into Buddhist Wisdom and the Natural World

Books by Bhikkhu Bodhi

Abhidhamma Studies
Buddhist Explorations of Consciousness and Time
(by Nyanaponika Thera, edited and introduced by Bhikkhu Bodhi)

The Connected Discourses of the Buddha
A Translation of the Saṃyutta Nikāya

Great Disciples of the Buddha
Their Lives, Their Works, Their Legacy
(by Nyanaponika Thera and Hellmuth Hecker,
edited by Bhikkhu Bodhi)

In the Buddha's Words
An Anthology of Discourses from the Pāli Canon

The Middle Length Discourses of the Buddha
A Translation of the Majjhima Nikāya
(translated by Bhikkhu Ñāṇamoli and Bhikkhu Bodhi)

The Numerical Discourses of the Buddha
A Complete Translation of the Aṅguttara Nikāya